Saga of
Direction

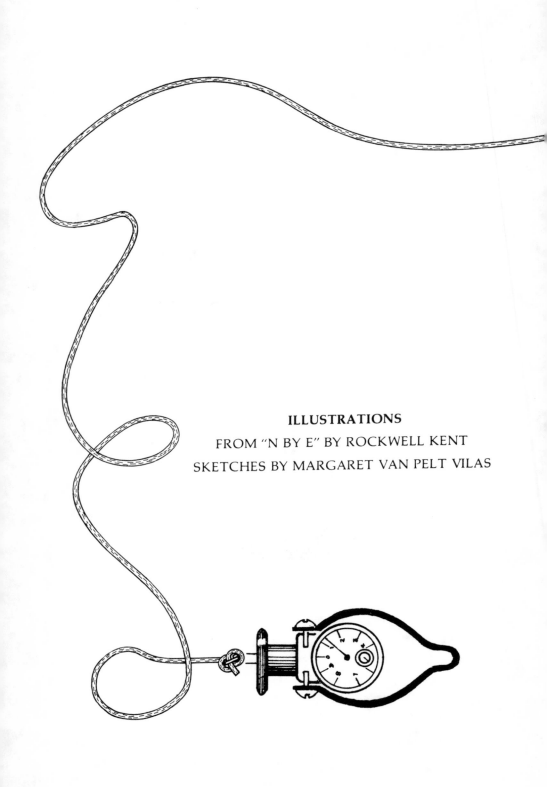

ILLUSTRATIONS

FROM "N BY E" BY ROCKWELL KENT

SKETCHES BY MARGARET VAN PELT VILAS

Saga of **DIRECTION**

by
CHARLES H. VILAS

INTRODUCTION BY
DR. MELVILLE BELL GROSVENOR

Seven Seas Press   New York N.Y.

FIRST EDITION

DEDICATION

This book is dedicated to the memory of
Arthur S. Allen Jr.
1907-1929
Classmate at Scarborough School, playmate and
neighbor, Philipse Manor, N.Y., 1918-1919, to
whom having a Direction in life was of sufficient
import to influence the naming of his boat.

Direction, *Lunenburg, 1946.*

CONTENTS

ILLUSTRATIONS

Woodcuts from N by E *by Rockwell Kent.*
Courtesy of the Rockwell Kent Legacies.

Sketches, line drawings by Margaret Van Pelt Vilas, A.W.S.
(Decorative sketches not listed)

PHOTOGRAPHS

MAPS & CHARTS

INTRODUCTION

Melville Bell Grosvenor

We were gathered aboard my yawl for a sundown gam when she made her entrance. In she swept, graceful and self-assured, drawing admiring glances from visiting yachtsmen who—like me— had anchored that afternoon in 1963 in Block Island's popular Great Salt Pond.

The lady looked vaguely familiar but I couldn't, for the life of me, recall where we might have met. Still puzzled, I turned back to my guests.

"*White Mist,* ahoy!"

An unexpected hail from alongside announced the arrival of a stocky stranger. Swinging effortlessly from dinghy to deck, he introduced himself as Charles "Carl" Vilas, whose name, a highly respected one in sailing circles, I had known for 30 years.

"Recognize her?" he asked, pointing at the trim cutter that had earlier caught my eye and challenged my memory. I admitted I couldn't place her.

"Look again."

Still, no luck.

"Why, that's *Direction,* Arthur Allen's old boat. Or was when I bought her back in 1946."

Then I remembered. Beautiful sunny days on the Bras d'Or Lakes of Cape Breton, Nova Scotia, where five generations of my family have spent their summers. From our place at Baddeck, I would often watch Arthur sail from his lone island hard on the wind with a fresh southerly blowing. Coming back and still hard on the wind, he could barely make his home mooring.

A dangerous situation, I thought: If a boat can't go to windward on a lee shore and has no engine, she can get into serious trouble which is nearly what happened to her on the west coast of New- foundland behind the Whale Rocks on her way to Greenland in

1929. Eventually a storm piled her onto others in a Greenland fjord, giving Allen's son and sometime-mariner Rockwell Kent a very close call with disaster. Fortunately, both crew and heavily damaged craft survived. In fact, Rockwell Kent went on to turn the voyage into an epic in his best seller *N by E*.

In those distant Bras d'Or days—and for years afterward—*Direction* was what is called a lubberly sailer. Patterned after the broad-beamed, wooden boats developed in Norway for rescue work, she was poorly rigged as an under-canvased sloop, clumsy, unable even to stand up to a brisk breeze. Yet, without motor, electricity, navigational aids, or any of the amenities associated with modern cruising, she managed a crossing of Davis Strait to Greenland, and made several round trips to Newfoundland with relative ease.

For, despite these handicaps, the lady had her points. Many a sailor—myself included—envied the clean lines of *Direction's* sleek, double-ended hull and the obvious seaworthiness of its design. It was that lack of windward ability that proved her Achilles' heel and limited her performance.

Only the hull could have stirred my feeling of familiarity as she slid into Great Salt Pond that day, slanting up to the wind at a jaunty heel. Otherwise, she had undergone a complete transformation. Now she was Marconi-rigged with tan mainsail and three roller-furling jibs. Moving saucily to her mooring, freshly painted, with everything shipshape and Bristol fashion, she reminded me of a debutante all dressed up and raring to go. And that's saying a lot for a damsel then close to 50 years old.

Credit for the new look and much-improved maneuverability goes, of course, to her skipper, who freely admits he lusted after the lady long before she became his. I'm sure even Margaret, Carl's charming wife and first mate, would agree that it's been a perfect match.

In correcting *Direction's* deficiencies, Carl converted her to an easily operated rig that enables him to set and furl his jibs from the cockpit, and to handle long cruises by himself. He's even licked the windward problem. "Don't look for me in a racing lineup; we're not quite up to that. But this old girl feeds to windward smartly enough to keep me out of trouble. She's comfortable, tight as a drum, and a completely reliable companion in almost any weather." A lot of praise for any ship.

Since our Block Island encounter, I have met Carl and *Direction* in many ports: at home base on Cape Breton's Washabuckt

River; Boulaceet Harbor; St. Pierre and Miquelon where we rafted up side by side and then explored the south coast of Newfoundland together. What a sight, what a delight to see that lovely waterbug beneath the magnificent, towering cliffs of Newfoundland's White River, and to realize she was the same cumbersome craft I used to watch thrashing across the Bras d'Or, going nowhere to windward.

Carl Vilas is a man of many parts. Long a member of the printing profession, he has been extremely active in the Cruising Club of America for some 40 years, holding numerous offices at both national and chapter level. A frequent contributor to the yachting press, he has served on the editorial staff of the *Cruising Club News* since its inception in 1962; he has been its able editor since 1975.

I have known many sailors in my life but never a better seaman and shipkeeper: *Direction* is as smartly turned out and carefully maintained as the best of the Bermuda racers. Though Carl can't stay with such fast company in competition, he's more than their match when gale winds rise and the going gets tough.

Here, this seasoned skipper adds to his considerable accomplishments by creating an extremely readable, briskly paced biography of a boat—his beloved *Direction*. She is, withal, a lady with a past well worth reporting. And, with Carl at the helm, the lady can certainly look forward to a lot of great years ahead.

M.B.G
Washington, D.C.
March 1977

Circa 1950

PREFACE

This is a browsing sort of book, to be opened at random for casual reading or perused from cover to cover, as your time or mood may dictate.

Picture yourself anchored in your boat near our cutter *Direction*, lying in some remote quiet harbor on a summer evening. I call a greeting across the water and you, accepting an invitation for a gam, row over, climb aboard and come below. With glass in hand you sit in *Direction's* cozy cabin, and we swap yarns.

Our common interest is obvious—boats. Should you be historically minded, I might reveal (without much persuasion) some tidbits of *Direction's* colorful background. If we discover we share technical interests, we might discuss details of *Direction's* ballast stowage or her roller-furling headsails. Or perhaps you are in a romantic mood and would enjoy hearing some anecdotes of *Direction's* travels to distant waters.

Direction, a scaled-down version of a Colin Archer *redningskoite*, or rescue boat, was launched in 1929 and, as you can see in her recent photos, she is still afloat in 1978—49 years later. She is known to many old timers and even quite a few younger sailors through Rockwell Kent's best seller of the early 1930's, *N by E*, a romantic chronicle of her cruise to Greenland and her shipwreck there in 1929. For many dreamers she has typified the ideal seagoing sailboat, and even today one runs across the name of Colin Archer in yachting magazines that promote fiberglass replicas of which *Direction* is a prototype. The current popularity of the Colin Archer design amounts to a backlash against the light-displacement, spade-rudder, fin-keel fashion of the 1970's. How justified these dreamers have been in selecting *Direction* as their ideal you may judge for yourself as you follow the vicissitudes which I, her owner, have faced for the past 31 years.

If you remain aboard long enough, I will introduce you to people who touched the life of *Direction* in one way or another over the years. To mention just a few who played leading roles in her story, there was Rockwell Kent, who sailed on her fateful voyage; Arthur S. Allen Jr., who was her original owner; Colin Archer himself, who never saw her, but was responsible for her lines; and the late Alfred F. Loomis, one of the more popular editors at *Yachting* for many years, who was the first to disillusion the dreamers by revealing *Direction's* shortcomings. There were many others who only step briefly on stage in her story, as exemplified by the following anecdote.

In July 1966 my wife and I had snugged *Direction* down to a heavy anchor in the Washabuckt River on the Bras d'Or Lakes of Nova Scotia. A hurricane located off Halifax was heading for Newfoundland. It was so far offshore that no more than gale warnings were posted locally, but rain was coming down in torrents. Clad in our oilskins, Margaret and I rowed ashore to do some shopping. As we entered the only store at Washabuckt Center, dripping with rain, a man spotted the name of our boat stenciled on our slickers.

"Oh, you are from *Direction*," he said. "I saw you last Sunday sailing into Baddeck. I know your boat well—recognized her when she was off Bienn Bhreagh. I haven't seen her in 20 years, but I would never mistake her. I have one of her logbooks at home, covering her passage from the states to Baddeck, back in 1932. Would you like to see it?"

My response was enthusiastic. "I'd love to see it," I said. "It must have been kept by a man named Ayres."

"So it was," he said,"Edward L. Ayres. I'll go home and get it."

Thus we met Joe "Red Rory" MacLean, owner and operator of the small ferry that plied between Lower Washabuckt and the county seat of Baddeck, one and a half miles across St. Patricks Channel.

When Mr. MacLean came aboard an hour later and presented me with the Ayres logbook—to keep!—our encounter was not only an interesting and happy one for me, but was also remarkable for being another in a series of events that might have been decreed by the Gods. During the years that Margaret and I have owned *Direction*, incidents of this sort, in which we have received artifacts relating to *Direction* or her story, have occurred with seemingly foreordained regularity. Stay with me and I shall describe other such incidents.

Direction's name and that of Rockwell Kent became linked in the minds of sailors and the general public during the early 1930's at a time when Kent was at the peak of his literary and artistic fame. *N by E* went through many editions. It struck a responsive chord in thousands of would-be adventurers struggling against the Promethean chains that bound them to mundane city lives. Result: A best seller, a happy publisher, and a boat that, despite questionable seaworthiness, became a symbol of romance and escape. Today such adventures are a dime a dozen, but in 1929 they were the stuff of high drama.

Manned by two 22-year-olds—Arthur S. Allen Jr., skipper, and Lucian Cary Jr., mate—plus 47-year-old Rockwell Kent, navigator, *Direction* sailed to Greenland without benefit of engine, radio, ballast or windward ability. Somehow she made it—but not all in one piece. After anchoring in her first Greenland fjord for the night, she was blown ashore the following morning by williwaws and pounded on the rocks until she was holed and sunk. Her crew got ashore and salvaged enough gear and food to survive. Kent trekked overland for two days and a night before reaching help. Later, after arrangements for repairing *Direction* had been made, Kent remained in Greenland to paint; Cary went to Paris; and Allen returned to his suburban home—only to be killed two weeks later by an auto as he stepped off a trolley car.

Direction was repaired by Greenlanders, shipped back to Philadelphia and sailed from there by Alfred Loomis of *Yachting* to his home on Long Island. The following summer, Edward L. Ayres delivered her to Arthur S. Allen Sr. at his vacation home in Baddeck, where he maintained her until his death in 1945.

My connection with *Direction* began remotely in Philipse Manor, New York, where in the winter of 1918-1919, "Art" Allen and I were schoolmates and chums. Our companionship lasted only that school year, because my family moved away the following summer, but it played its part in my acquisition of *Direction* many years later.

In 1945 I needed a larger boat, having for 20 years sailed a catboat in which I dared not to go to sea. Like many others I had followed the romantic career of *Direction* and regarded her as my ideal craft. Because of this and my early friendship with young Art Allen, I had kept in touch with his father. So, on his death I found where *Direction* was, and purchased her from the Allen estate through the Pinaud Yacht Yard in Baddeck. Many of the unseaworthy aspects of *Direction* had been corrected by

Walter Pinaud before I bought her. We were satisfied that she was safe to take to sea when we arrived for her delivery cruise to Connecticut in July of 1946.

"Why would you want a boat like *Direction?*" I have been asked by many friends. "She's slow to windward, heavier than you will ever need on Long Island Sound, and you never can win a race in her." I find it just as hard to give a logical reply as did her original owner trying to explain why he would have neither engine nor radio aboard. It's a matter of personality and temperament. Some of the pleasures of yachting are enjoyed vicariously, and to own a boat in which you *could* sail around the world, or to Greenland if you had the time and money, is a source of satisfaction, though you may never leave your home waters. For 20 years, as a matter of fact, those aforementioned Promethean chains kept me and *Direction* west of Cape Cod. But they were 20 happy years, raising a family, earning a living, sailing *Direction* in the summer—and eliminating rot in the winter.

There is some sort of "Gresham's Law" concerning old wooden boats that I can't clearly define, which relates to rot, upkeep and the lifespan of a boat. When rot rears its ugly head, the owner sells the boat to a "bargain hunter" who can ill afford to make repairs after stretching his pocketbook merely to buy it. So rot grows worse, the boat is sold again to someone even more impecunious, and in a few years she is ready for the boneyard. The old boats that are still in good shape remain so because they are in the hands of owners who are willing and able to keep up with the ravages of time. My repair bills over the years would easily have purchased more than one modern fiberglass yacht—had such been what I wanted.

There comes a time when you begin to wonder if you will ever sail to the faraway land of your dreams. Delay too long and dry rot may invade your own joints and arteries and incapacitate you for that day which you keep postponing. It may be later than you think. And so, with our retirement just over the horizon, we sailed back to Nova Scotia in 1966 to base *Direction* off some waterfront land we had just purchased. That is how we happened to be at anchor in the Washabuckt River on the day when the Gods brought us together with Joe MacLean, to continue a series of apparently predestined events that have added so much to the rewards of owning *Direction*.

Pour yourself another dram and settle down while I take you back to 1929, and tell you the full, romantic saga of *Direction*.

xviii

ACKNOWLEDGMENTS

For nearly half a century my wife, Margaret, and I have shared many common interests, not the least of which has been the owning of *Direction*. We have collaborated in other fields, however, and this book is an example. Without her sketch pad and pencil I simply would not have had the inspiration to compile and write it. So it is understandable, I am certain, why I put her name first in my list of thanks. Without her skills, abilities, humor and tolerance, life for me might have been a rather dull experience.

Melville Bell Grosvenor has taken time out from a busy and important schedule to read my manuscript and write a most appropriate introduction. Nobody living could be better qualified for the task regardless of who might be the author of the book.

A book of this nature, which is in part an anthology, results from the generosity and interest of many people. Much of its theme is based upon that fact. Were it not for the editors of *Yachting, Sail,* and *Cruising World,* the saga of *Direction* could not have been presented in the words of those who were there. Similarly, Rockwell Kent's widow, Sally, and her husband, John F.H. Gorton, have put the Rockwell Kent Legacies at my disposal so that appropriate woodcuts from *N by E* could decorate these pages. They also supplied the photograph of Rockwell Kent aboard the *Lonsdale* in the Straits of Magellan, a rare and happy pose of more than fifty years ago. Robert S. Carter and his wife, Cynthia, went out of their way to visit Larvik Fjord and the home of Colin Archer, and record for these pages one more facet of the remarkable saga of *Direction*—they deserve my thanks, too.

People such as the Reverend Lewis H. Davis, Peggy and Harry Calnan, and Joseph MacLean, are mentioned at length in the text, but others who made contributions should be thanked here as well, including Joseph P. Blair III, who supplied the photograph appearing on the front of the dust jacket, Robert L. Hall, who snapped the photo of me which appears elsewhere on the dust jacket, and Margery Blair Perkins who took the photo on the back of the dust jacket. Bill Hartman, Robert Hartwell Moore, W. Perry Curtiss, John Atkin, John E. Barbour, Peter Barlow, Jan Wilsgaard, Andrew J. Lindsay, Stuart Hotchkiss, and Allen Richardson also supplied photographs to add to the interest of this book.

Margaret Joyce, my copy editor, and long-time mentor Steve Doherty of Seven Seas Press, took file and rasp in hand to smooth off (hopefully) most of the rough edges of my prose, for which I am eternally grateful. Rudolph Ruzicka, a long-time friend of Rockwell Kent and a world-renowned artist in his own right, made the map for *Under Sail to Greenland* which I have reproduced in these pages. Clayton Slawter painted the picture of *Shanghai,* a photo of which was given to me by Frederick Jay Wells, earning my gratitude. David Stephens Traxel, Rockwell Kent's biographer, and John Leather, Colin Archer's biographer, both shared with me valuable information of mutual use.

There have been others who sent me old clippings pertaining to *Direction,* Andrew J. Lindsay being one example, whose names have escaped me, but to whom I am indebted.

Without Leif R. Lund, Secretary General of the Norsk *Selskab Til Skibbrudnes Redning,* and the help of the editor of their publication, *Redningsselskapet,* Kjell Gabrielsen, I never would have obtained the rare photos reproduced here, and the Xerox copy of *Colin Archer: A Memoir,* by James Archer, upon which I based my information about the famous designer of *redningskoites.*

Sohei Hohri, librarian at the New York Yacht Club, demonstrated that the computer is still no substitute for an alert brain when he produced the most amazing references to Colin Archer in Norsk and English from the uncatalogued files at his command. Walter B. Gallagher, Administrative Assistant for the Society of Naval Architects and Marine Engineers, was able to supply me with information concerning Archer's Wave Form Theory. Naval Architect William Garden also responded most helpfully to my inquiries about Billy Atkin, John Hanna, and Colin Archer, while Professor Asger H. Aaboe of Yale made some very helpful translations. Sigurd Bane sent me much useful literature concerning the Colin Archer Club of Stockholm.

And, of course, this book never would have been written but for the fact that *Direction* is still around in the flesh. She would long since have been recycled had not personal interest far beyond the call of duty been lavished on her by Seth Persson (who carved her wood tiller), Bill and Ken Bedell of Bedell's Shipyard in Stratford, Connecticut, Jack Jacques and his high-morale crew of the Dutch Wharf Boatyard in Branford, Connecticut, and finally, for the past eleven years, the Pinaud family in Baddeck, Nova Scotia : Fred, Ralph, Muriel, and their late father, Walter. Without these dedicated people and their loyal staff, there would today be no *Direction* to write about. I thank them all.

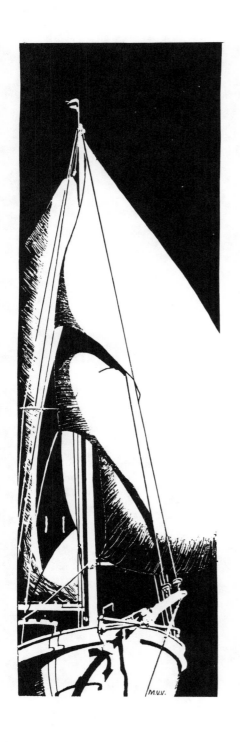

PART I:
The Sagas

AN ADVENTUROUS CRUISE — AND THE CREW WHICH WILL MAKE IT
By Lucius Beebe
(1929)

AUTHOR'S NOTE: Cruising in the 1970's is vastly different from what it was in the 1920's and 1930's. Before World War II and the population explosion among boats the announcement of an impending cruise to northern waters—or any distant sea—was almost certain to produce editorial interest in both newspapers and yachting magazines. It was not uncommon for such ventures to be preceded by somewhat boastful press releases. They could spark instant and unearned fame. Frequently when Father Neptune got wind of them he retaliated just to show who was boss in his domain.

What follows is a press release that appeared in the July 1929 issue of Yachting, *written by the prestigious Lucius Beebe, and instigated by Rockwell Kent's publicity minded publisher, much to the chagrin of* Direction's *owner, Arthur (Sam) Allen Jr., who understood full well how such bragging might sit with Father Neptune.*

Rockwell Kent, well known as an author and an artist, is also an adventurer. At various times in an eventful career he has crossed the Atlantic in a ketch with only two companions; he has spent an icebound winter in Alaska in search of artistic and literary material, and has courted adventure in the distant, uncharted seas of Tierra del Fuego in a condemned lifeboat, refitted and strengthened for ocean sailing.

Now the urge to wander has come upon him again. From his studio high in the Adirondacks he metaphorically sniffs the salt tang of the North Atlantic, and June will find him setting sail from Baddeck, Cape Breton, in quest of the shores of far-off Greenland.

The crew will consist of himself, Arthur S. Allen Jr., the captain and a student of naval architecture at the Massachusetts Institute of Technology, and Lucian Cary Jr., of Winsted, Connecticut, whose father is the well-known short story writer. Like Kent, both Allen and Cary are experienced sailors, so that, as in the song, "no wind that blew dismayed her crew or troubled the captain's mind."

A boat exactly suited to their needs was found on the ways at Miller's Shipyard, in Nyack, New York. She had been designed originally for a cruise in the South Seas, but circumstances forced her first owner to abandon his project, and *Direction* was purchased by Allen's father, Arthur S. Allen, of New York City, who completely rebuilt and outfitted her for sailing in northern waters. *Direction* is an adaptation by M. H. Miner of Colin Archer's original design for a 47-foot Norwegian rescue-boat. A double-ended, cutter-rigged boat, 33 feet long, she is built throughout of the finest selected white oak, and her construction is practically double the strength of that required for safety in a boat her size. She has no motor, both because of a prejudice against such modernities on the part of the 20th-century Argonauts who are to navigate her, and because it was felt that too much speed might drive her upon unseen floating ice. Her cabin can accommodate three passengers in comfort and her cruising range, limited only by her capacity for the storage of food and water, is, to all intents and purposes, unlimited. She is particularly adapted to cruising in ice-infested waters, and is considered one of the safest of all types of boats for heavy weather.

Because of the abbreviated summer vacations of the two college men, the trip from New York to Cape Breton will be made some time previous to the cruise proper, which is scheduled to begin promptly the first week in June. From Baddeck, *Direction* will sail north through the Gulf of St. Lawrence and the Straits of Belle Isle, down the Labrador coast, and over the open sea to Greenland, the ultimate objective of the voyage being the vicinity of Godhavn, or even farther north. The open-water voyage, by the route now under consideration, is something over 600 miles, although the entire trip will require something over 5000 miles, and it is expected that the eastward passage will take five to six weeks, the trip home consuming a longer period because of the less favorable prevailing winds. Sufficient stores will be taken aboard for a voyage far longer than that anticipated, and no delays will cause the adventurers any uneasiness on this account.

The cruise, it is planned, will take about three months, unless, as Kent says almost wistfully, it should be prolonged by adverse winds or bad weather. There is no scientific purpose behind the trip and no precise destination. "To invent a purpose, other than the quest of literary and artistic material," says Kent, "would be sheerest rationalization."

DIRECTION *off the coast of Greenland,*
from a woodcut by Rockwell Kent.

A SUMMER CRUISE TO GREENLAND
By Arthur S. Allen Jr.
(1929)

AUTHOR'S NOTE: This story appeared in Yachting *magazine shortly after the tragic death of Arthur S. Allen Jr. Direction's cruise had ended on the rocks of a Greenland fjord, Allen had returned home, and had nearly completed this story when he was struck down by an automobile.*

Direction *was the third yacht ever to sail to Greenland. She also was the third to be shipwrecked for none had returned safely. All three were basically of the same design—Colin Archer redningskoites or "rescue-boats." The other two boats were* Leiv Eriksson, *which disappeared after departing from Greenland in 1924, and* Shanghai, *which was wrecked on the coast of Nova Scotia after having visited Greenland in 1924. Rockwell Kent had originally planned to make the 1924 voyage aboard* Shanghai, *but had backed out at the last moment. Here is young Sam Allen's story:*

Lucian Cary Jr.

"But why Greenland? The West Indies would be good and the Mediterranean even better—but Greenland! Oh, well, I'll go with you, just this once."

This was the condescending message which came from Europe last spring, completing the crew of the cutter *Direction*. There were then three of us, the whole ship's company, and the worst of the complications of preparation for the cruise were complete.

Rockwell Kent, artist and wanderer, had signed on earlier in the winter, anxious to go because of his natural taste for such an expedition, coupled with his desire to paint in Greenland; and Lucian Cary, who "would rather make it the West Indies," came home from Paris in the spring. Both men had those rare qualities necessary for a voyage in a small ship under sail alone, and as I found later, I could not possibly have chosen better companions. Cary had cruised with me before.

Direction is a 13¾-ton cutter. She was designed by M. H. Miner of New York, who followed the principles of Colin Archer in his design, turning out a 33-footer with the easy, fair lines of the Norwegian lifesaving boats, some of which are still in use in the North Sea. The ship was originally intended to take Mr. Miner to the Pacific, but complications caused this project to be abandoned. So she came into my hands, in an unfinished state, in a small yard at Nyack-on-the-Hudson.

With a Greenland cruise in mind, the greatest care was exercised in her completion, and though the yachtsman's usual difficulties in getting work done well and on time were encountered, she was finally launched, rigged and pronounced seaworthy. She was well designed, well built and properly fitted out. Her construction was heavier than is usual and her standing rigging was brutal. Larsen made the sails, and they were tanned, a practice common in Europe.

Stores, supplies and instruments were gathered under the direction of Rockwell Kent, who immediately proved that he knew what he was about. The Hamilton Watch Company loaned two fine chronometer watches which had been used on an expedition to the Gobi Desert, and we were offered a fine radio receiving set, but I refused this—amid a storm of protest from friends.

My decision to leave the radio at home was based on reasons somewhat analogous to those which made me decide to do without a motor, and the explanation is completely incomprehensible to most people, sailors included. I feel that my dislike of motors is sufficient justification for not using one; but, if necessary, I can

7

make it clear that I do not need one. We did not have room for an engine, or its fuel; the crew's full time was needed for handling sail; and I dislike the noise of a motor when approaching land, ships or whistle buoys in the fog. Leif Ericsson did it without a "kicker," so did Magellan—but here I begin to run into inconsistencies. Those gentlemen also got along without special logs, ship's bell clocks and canned whole squab, all of which I took with me.

However, those of us who cruise without power are in an ever-increasing minority. Some of our best sailors have been lost in craft with engines and without them, and though he who has power will probably less often be in a delicate situation involving danger, he will also be less able to cope with such difficulty when it arises.

Finally completed, fitted out and with all necessary supplies and instruments aboard, *Direction* left New York late in May 1929 bound for Bras d'Or Lakes, Cape Breton, Nova Scotia. Mr. Cary was in command, and had with him Joseph Murphy, an experienced sailor from Cape Breton Island, as the writer was still busy at M.I.T. The passage was made without undue difficulty, but with no great speed before the summer sou'west breezes which blow off our coast. They reported that the ship had proved herself very handy, and that with a free wind, she was very fast indeed. But no weather sufficiently boisterous to constitute a test of her seaworthiness was encountered.

At Baddeck, where I joined the ship early in June, we hauled out near Casey Baldwin's yard for paint. The work done there is always prompt and good, and we spent the next week checking gear, stowing and making final preparation for sea.

The sailing date was set for June 17, and by that time all was in readiness. We cleared at 4:30, with a beautiful westerly blowing across the bay from the hills, and those on the dock saw us run out and around the point in short order. The wind lightened somewhat presently, but we ran out of the Bras d'Or Lakes in six hours. Then the wind hauled to the north and freshened.

The log was streamed and a departure was taken with Cibaux Island abeam, course NE, distance 100 miles to Cape Anguille, Newfoundland. The wind headed us a bit, freshening through the night until we were hove-to under staysail at 10 o'clock the next morning. It was a good solid breeze of wind from the north but, still, we could have carried on had it not been a headwind. *Direction* is no flyer to weather, and when it blows from that quarter it is easier for all concerned to heave her to and jog along under

8

DIRECTION *hauled out at Casey Baldwin's boatyard, Baddeck,
Nova Scotia, just prior to her departure for Greenland, 1929.*

Log: Yacht, "Direction"

From: Baddeck, C.B.   To: Port aux Basques, Newfoundland

TIME	LOG	CHART COURSE	COURSE STEERED	WIND	BAR.	THER.	
							June 17, 1929
4:35 p.m.	—	S E	S E	W by N	29.99	78	Cleared Baddeck.
10:10 p.m.	—	N E ½ E	N E	N N W	29.98	66	Out of lakes and on course across Cabot Strait. Log streamed to Cibaux I. abeam to port 2 miles. At P M log, course N E, dist. 100 miles to C. Anguille to haul to starboard.
10:30 p.m.	33.6	48 deg.	N E	N N W	29.98	66	5.5 knots — not bad.
11:30 p.m.	39.1	"	"	"	"	"	
							June 18, 1929
1:10 a.m.	46.0	N E	E N E	N by E	29.9	56	Wind dropped — then headed.
4:20 a.m.	60.5	N E	N E	N by W	"	"	Fresh breeze.
10:15 a.m.							Hove to under staysail. Breeze too heavy for working to N E conveniently. Rockwell gives 1 at 46 deg. 55' 20" at noon. My fix for 1:00 P M 46 deg. 55' — 59 deg. 41'. Drift E by S (73 deg. true) 2 knots.
4:00 p.m.							Set double reef main and full headsails. Four knots N E by E from 46 deg. 57' — 59 deg. 34'

Sample pages from *DIRECTION'S* log book.
Above, from *UNDER SAIL TO GREENLAND.*
Opposite page, from actual log in Allen's handwriting.

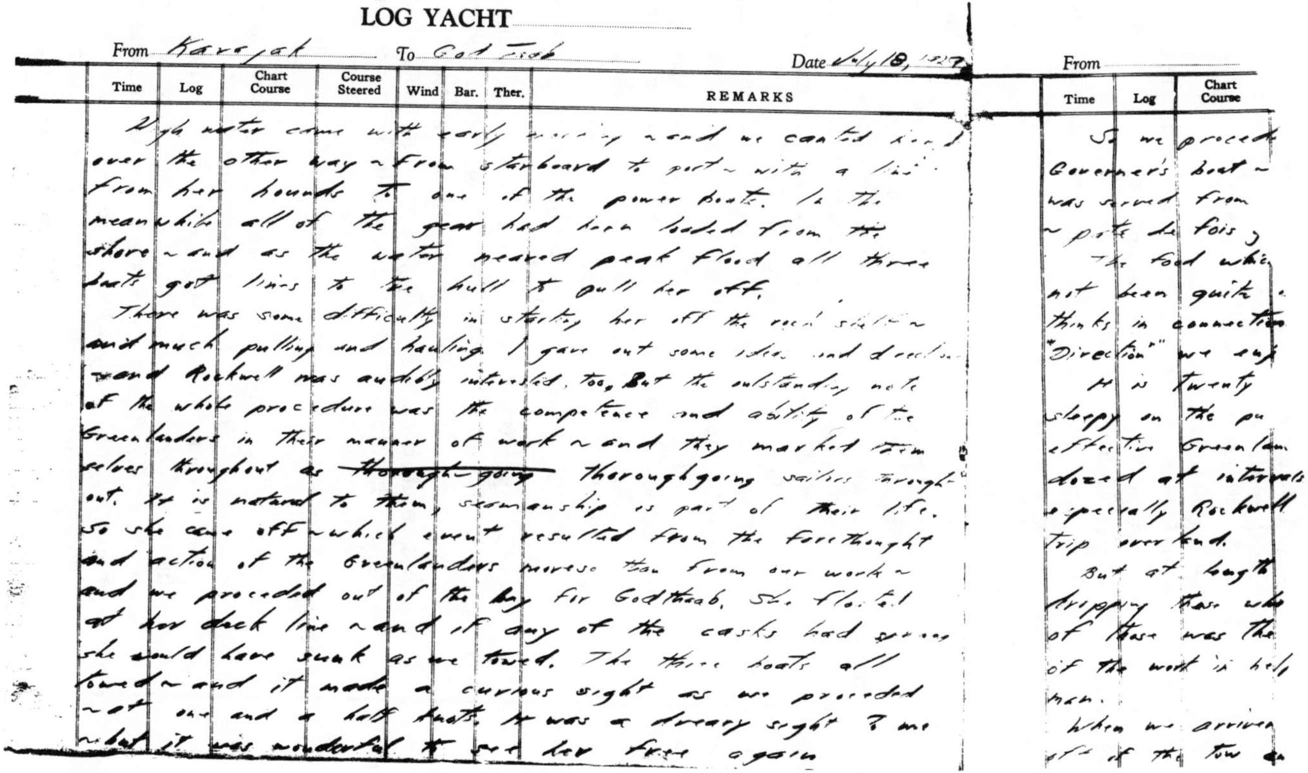

LOG YACHT

From Karajak To Godthaab Date July 18, 1929

Time	Log	Chart Course	Course Steered	Wind	Bar.	Ther.	REMARKS

High water came with early morning – and we canted her over the other way – from starboard to port – with a line from her hounds to one of the power boats. In the meanwhile all of the gear had been loaded from the shore – and as the water neared peak flood all three boats got lines to the hull to pull her off.

There was some difficulty in starting her off the rock shelf – and much pulling and hauling. I gave out some ideas and directions – and Rockwell was audibly interested, too. But the outstanding note of the whole procedure was the competence and ability of the Greenlanders in their manner of work – and they marked them selves throughout as ~~thorough-going~~ thoroughgoing sailors throughout. It is natural to them, seamanship is part of their life. So she came off – which event resulted from the forethought and action of the Greenlanders moreso than from our work – and we proceeded out of the bay for Godthaab. She floated at her deck line – and if any of the casks had sprung she would have sunk as we towed. The three boats all towed – and it made a curious sight as we proceeded – at one and a half knots. It was a dreary sight to me – but it was wonderful to see her free again

From

Time	Log	Chart Course

So we proceed
Governor's boat –
was served from
– pâté de fois
The food whic
not been quite
thinks in connection
"Direction" we enj
It is twenty
sleepy on the pu
effective Greenlan
dozed at intervals
especially Rockwell
trip overland.
But at length
dropping those who
of these was the
of the work is help
man.
When we arrived

short canvas, provided there is sea room and time. She is stiff and dry, but her speed on the wind is slow, and her leeway great. However, give her two points free, and on any course from that to a dead run she is the fastest, most able cruising boat of her size I have ever seen. She steers very easily indeed, and can carry on long after other small ships are in danger because of their own speed and the sea which makes up.

In the afternoon we set double-reefed main and full headsails, and proceeded to Newfoundland a bit to the eastward of our course, making a landfall soon after midnight at Cape Ray. Then it began to blow—really blow.

As we were in a hurry to get up the Straits of Belle Isle, and to the Labrador, we started a hard grind to windward. It was a dead headwind of gale velocity, but we challenged it, still under double-reefed main and full headsails. *Direction* took a beating and did very well indeed. There we learned that she was strong. For a while we took the staysail off, but it did not ease her much, and at one time her starboard running light, screen and all, six feet above the deck, was rolled under water. It was foolish to carry on; the ship was too small to make much headway to weather against such wind and seas, and that evening we ran her into Port aux Basques, Newfoundland. The fishermen there were surprised that we had bucked the gale, for which they evidently had great respect. They were not accustomed to such weather in summer and one of their schooners offshore had needed assistance.

After the gale came calm. When we worked out of the harbor and around Cape Ray the breeze was light, variable and uncertain. As far as progress was concerned, this was worse than the gale, but at length it came from astern, which was pleasant—but for the fact that it brought fog. We had been told by schooner captains in Port aux Basques that we need expect no fog on the west coast of Newfoundland, but, as it turned out, it was thick as pea soup all the way.

And we nearly lost the ship, too, as a result of a careless error in this fog. We got about five miles off our reckoning on the land side, as a result, I think, of leaving an iron bucket too near the binnacle. This introduced an error of nearly half a point. It was very thick and we were doing five knots under spinnaker in my watch that afternoon. Suddenly, rocks appeared on the starboard bow. We were approaching too close to land and had to take in the spinnaker and jibe the mainsail to stand out to sea. This was all

12

Arthur S. (Sam) Allen at the helm of DIRECTION
*just before making the landfall on the coast
of Greenland, 1929.*

very well until we got the spinnaker off her. But then rocks appeared to *port* also! We had run into a nest of them, charted five or six miles offshore. A large, steep sea was running, and to hit anything solid that far offshore, in that fog, would have been worse than embarrassing. With the spinnaker off and the rocks on either beam now close, I considered the situation for a brief interval. At this juncture came the report of rocks dead ahead as well! This forced the decision to turn back immediately. The question of the moment (we were then doing four knots) was whether to shove the tiller hard down and take the chance that she would not miss stays (if she did we would be driven on to the rocks, now close, originally seen to starboard), or to wear, which she would do slowly, and get on the starboard tack in that manner.

Choosing the latter alternative, I threw the tiller hard up. At first she just drove on, without falling away to starboard; we now had about 300 feet to go, at four knots, to the rocks ahead over which the seas were dashing magnificently. Then she began to wear, faster and faster, until we jibed her all standing; then we began to trim as if there were a $1000 note fastened insecurely to the clew of the mainsail, and she began to forge ahead. As I have said, she is slow on the wind, and not quick in stays. We

13

Channel
Port au Basques } Nfld.   June 21st A.M.

[1929]

My darlings:

    / DO .   / do '

/ do !

    For 36 hours weve been a
board — after weathering the worst gale
theyve had on this coast for
ages   our ships lights were under
water

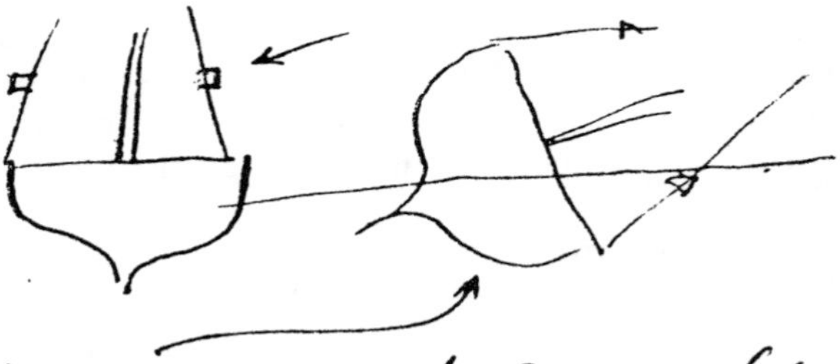

    Like that.   I saved her
deal through it all.
    I love you all in all — but
its a good thing youre not along
        Yr
        R.

June 21st A.M.

Channel
Port au Basques   Newfoundland

[1929]

My darling,

I do!   I do!

I do!

       For 36 hours we've been a-
board — after weathering the worst gale
they've had on this coast for
ages. Our ship's lights were under
water

    Like this.   I served hot
meals through it all.
     I love you all in all — but
it's a good thing you're not along.
         Yours
          R.

This letter was uncovered by Rockwell Kent's biographer, David Traxel, during his research at the Smithsonian Institution. It was written in Newfoundland shortly before Direction sailed for Greenland. "I do! I do! I do!" was Kent's private code with Frances, his second wife, and was used as well in his transatlantic cables. It originated from her question, "Do you love me?" Wife #1 was Kathleen, for whom he named the lifeboat he sailed in the Straits of Magellan, and Wife #3 was Sally.

made six hitches, each one ending with the sight of rocks ahead. But at last, on a seaward hitch, we came clear and the bowsprit watch went below to serve out rum. That incident was rank carelessness, and we were lucky.

The fog held another day, but the wind left us in the middle of the Straits where we got a fair fix by the Greenly Island fog signal. Then, when it cleared, we saw our first ice, and though at first it was not very impressive, there was more to come. The wind headed us, the fog rolled away completely, and we gave up a long windward thrash to Forteau Bay, Labrador, in favor of a short run to leeward to Bradore Bay, Quebec. We ran in before a gale of wind in the early morning. Here we lay at anchor for two days, and then spent the better part of two more outside, waiting for wind. When the wind finally came, there was too much of it. We left Greenly Island astern, after seeing our first whales, but were soon forced into St. Clair Bay on a rising north-easter. This is on the southern end of the Labrador coast. We found a good anchorage and were glad to be safe in port in what proved to be a very dirty night, with the wind whining aloft and Eskimo dogs howling ashore. The gale held all next day.

Although we were impatient with these delays, we found much to interest us. The coast here is high, barren and desolate, but there is a stern grandeur about it, with mountains ashore and large bergs out in the Straits. The people, who live a dreary life, were pleased to see us and visited in large numbers. They all wanted cigarettes, razor blades, medical supplies, etc., and we gave them what we could spare. Some of the children helped clean up the ship in return for bits of strawberry jam, candy or dimes.

We managed to be comfortable aboard the boat. Kent and Cary are accomplished cooks, as well as reliable sailors, and lightened the hours with good meals. We ate much seal meat which we got from fishermen, and this proved to be fine food. One of our best common dishes was brewis, a Newfoundland dish, which is hard bread soaked overnight, fried and served with molasses, a good dish, and easy to prepare.

At 3:30 the following day we got under way again, with mostly clear weather and a light northwest wind. We sailed through the night, under spinnaker part of the time, and in the morning were running along at six knots with a fair wind. We arrived early at Battle Harbour, Labrador, where we were towed through a very narrow pass, with steep rocks 10 feet to port. Our pilot was good, and needed to be.

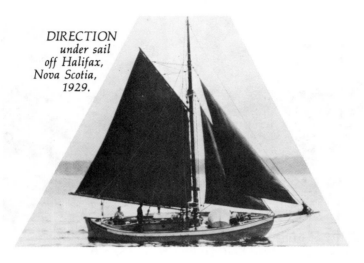

DIRECTION
under sail
off Halifax,
Nova Scotia,
1929.

The next two days we spent visiting the Grenfell mission, replenishing our coal, wood, water and kerosene, and cleaning ship. It was on the second day here that we had our experience with an iceberg. I happened to stick my head out the hatch and noticed, about 100 feet away, a large berg bearing down on our anchorage. It was about 70 feet by 50 and stood seven feet out of water. Action seemed called for. We got out of its way by working around it, but nearly lost an anchor. You have to stay on the job on this coast.

On July 5, at 3:00 A.M., we sailed out of Battle Harbour for Godthaab, Greenland, full of anticipation and interest as to how *Direction* would weather the long stretch of open water. It was a great relief to leave the Straits, with their unfavorable winds and floating ice, for the open sea. We had decided on Godthaab as our objective, as it is the capital of southern Greenland and one of the few towns of any size in the country. It is well up the west coast of Greenland, and we hoped after landing there to continue on to Godhavn and the Arctic Circle. Then, on the way home, we planned to sail westward to northern Labrador, perhaps up to Baffin Land, and down to Newfoundland again. On the return voyage we expected to go outside of Newfoundland, as we decided the Straits take too much time.

17

At anchor in Battle Harbour, Labrador, 1929.
Left to right: *Rockwell Kent, Lucian Cary and Sam Allen.*

Our course out of Battle Harbour was N by E and we were making about six knots in a southwest wind, with the spinnaker set. We had to allow 15 miles setback for the Labrador current. A thick fog came on at evening, and we checked our position frequently.

The next day, after using the spinnaker in the morning, we struck a dead calm in the afternoon, but on the following day we passed the iceberg line, with all clear ahead to Greenland. So far the voyage was uneventful, with *Direction* standing up well. Three days out from shore we passed a spherical buoy bound with rope, one foot in diameter, which puzzled us. Otherwise there was no sign of life. We found that on our northeast course we were getting too far to the eastward, so that we had to make it NE by N when possible.

The weather had been cold and dirty, and in the afternoon it breezed up from W by N, with a short, nasty sea making up. This increased, so that at 2:00 A.M. we hove-to under staysail with main and jib stowed. Our drift was about 1.5 knots ESE. By 5:30 A.M. we were able to put the double-reefed main on and continue our course. All day it blew hard.

By midnight we had shaken out the reefs and had a light favorable wind, but a confused sea which we knew would be with us for a long time. We set the spinnaker at 2:30 A.M. and started to buck into the head swell. But the wind increased again and was really blowing by the time I next came on watch. I hung on as

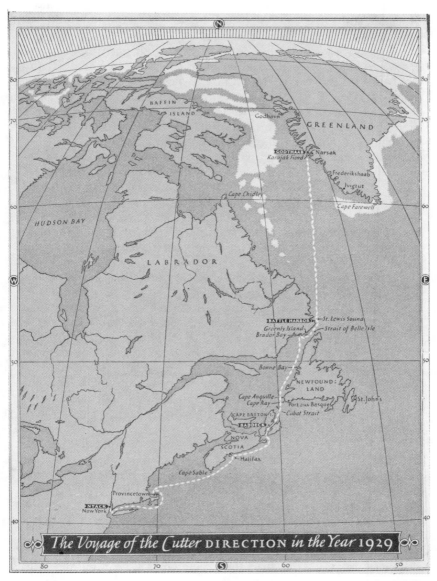

The Voyage of the Cutter DIRECTION in the Year 1929

This map was designed and drawn by Rudolph Ruzicka, a prominent artist whose works are found in many galleries today. Ruzicka was a personal friend both of Rockwell Kent and Arthur S. Allen Sr., and this map was his contribution to UNDER SAIL TO GREENLAND, the book Mr. Allen's friends lovingly produced to memorialize his son.

long as I dared, too long, up to seven knots, with 40 knots or more of wind, under full sail. At 3:30 P.M. it was a full gale and we took in the main and jib and hove-to.

Next morning we were under way again, but our troubles were not over. As we were proceeding with the main on, the port gaff jaw broke off short. We worked fast lowering the mainsail and managed not to rip it. Kent did a good job of making a new gaff jaw out of the spare tiller, while I set spinnaker and jib, and we kept off under that and headsails for the four hours it took to get the main on again. We now had a good breeze abeam, with smooth water and only a moderate swell. We sighted a steam trawler to weather—our first encounter since leaving Battle Harbour.

July 12, seven days out, we were beating to windward in a breeze which we hoped would not increase, when some small ice, weeds and two small sea birds prepared us for the cry of "Land Ho!" It was thick, with visibility one-half mile, but we made out rocks to leeward. The water, too, was now a jade color instead of deep blue. We tacked out to sea again, having covered about 666 miles. The next problem was to find a good anchorage.

The next two days were difficult ones. The fog held, and it was impossible to get a meridian altitude or recognize the shoreline. It was very cold on deck, and all we could do was beat up the coast, close to shore, with two reefs in the main, waiting for it to clear. The wind was southerly, bringing more fog. Several times we had to go about when rocks appeared close aboard.

All the morning of July 14 it stayed pea soup thick, and we lowered the main and jib and proceeded downwind under staysail. The wind then freshened and finally it began to clear. We decided to jog in and look it over.

With the lifting of the fog we had our first full view of the beautiful Greenland coast, and it was worth coming twice that far to see. We ran along to the north and after much guessing picked up some day beacons placed on large rocks. With Kent going over the charts and Cary at the masthead, we finally developed our position as approaching Godthaab Fjord from the south. Shaking out the reefs and setting the spinnaker, we went along very fast. But everything is so majestically large on this coast that the distances prove greater than they seem. In a light rain, and with some confusion below, where the crew was at the charts, as to the nature of the land ahead, we decided to run into a small fjord for the night, as it was dirty outside and we still had 18 miles to go.

20

Rockwell Kent

SHIPWRECK

This Greenland fjord, our first anchorage after our run across from the Labrador, was a lovely one. There were huge, steep mountains completely surrounding us, with freshwater streams splashing down, a few sandy beaches and large overhanging glaciers. The whole harbour was but a mile long and a quarter-mile wide. We seemed completely protected, with the holding ground good.

But we did not know Greenland. Early next morning we were nearly thrown out of our bunks by a terrific blast of wind which hove the ship down, rail under. A succession of these followed, first one side, then the other. In half an hour *Direction* took a knockdown puff from abeam which hove her down on her beam ends, under bare poles, at anchor, so that water poured down the main hatch.

21

*Wrecked in Karajak Fjord. These photos were
made from frames taken from Rockwell Kent's
16mm movie, shot during the storm.*

She started to drag. We payed out more cable and also let go the heavy anchor. The surface of the water was a thick mass of flying white scud which cut one's face like a charge of rock salt. Faster she dragged, pulling her two anchors through the sand, so fast that they could not even hold her head to it. The rocks to leeward were only 300 or 400 feet off and we got out our last anchor. The spare and the chain were ready, and a sounding about 75 feet from shore showed plenty of water, but we saw that it was already too late. The third anchor would not be ready in time.

A few feet from the rocks she stopped to consider, or else fate gave her a moment to say her last words, so to speak. Her two hooks caught and brought her head to it, where she rode for a minute or two. Then she broke them out again, and the seas, now large for only a half-mile fetch, drove her to the jagged ledge, which rose from deep water at about a 45-degree angle. She struck with a horrible crash, and then the elements went to work on her in earnest.

I tried to get a tackle from her masthead to the shore, while Kent and Cary collected supplies we would need. They had a bad time below, with the crashers shaking her frame every few seconds, but they managed to get many things ashore during the short time we had, though I could do little with the masthead line. It was wonderful how she withstood annihilation for the first few minutes, with no water appearing below, but soon she was holed in two or three places, and filled and sank to her deck level, where she rested on the rocks.

She had been stiff and powerful enough to come to Greenland, weathering two gales, only to be wrecked in harbour! At sea we could probably have lasted out the storm. But what had happened was that the high wind which had helped us into the fjord had developed into a gale, and the sea opening acted as a funnel to lend the wind a tremendous force. It hit the ship squarely, and once we started dragging there was no help for us.

Once on shore we found a lee to bring our stores to and made camp on the rocks, with the spinnaker rigged as a lean-to. We made it as comfortable as we could, with everything wet, and walked about to keep warm. The gale was still blowing off the mountains, and to leeward of us the waterfalls, instead of dropping down from crag to crag, went straight *up* the mountains, and dispersed as mist, giving an effect of smouldering fires, uncanny and beautiful. Out in the harbour, sheets of white water still blanketed the surface, and tiny water spouts rose here and there where the wind whirled.

23

The wind and rain lasted all day, but toward night it took off and we decided to get further supplies from the wreck. *Direction* was a forlorn sight, battered and broken, with a heavy list, her mainmast and all standing rigging standing into the sky as firmly as the day she was launched. Below she was a complete wreck. Drawers, tables, shelves, bulkheads and doors were torn away and scrambled together under the cabin top. We managed to save a few things floating in this mass and to hook up some things from the depths of the water with the fish gaff. We had enough food for quite a while, and collected much wood from the wreck, as there is none in this country.

Kent, who is resourceful and accustomed to wild country, started out next morning to find a settlement, while Cary and I kept camp and continued salvage work. Kent equipped himself with enough food for a few days—soup, chocolate, etc. Among the things we had saved was a chart which showed a settlement five or 10 miles to the north, but we had no way of knowing whether it was accessible from the spot where we had landed. Godthaab, about 20 miles by water, could not be made without a boat, and if Kent were not successful in finding help we planned to try to do something with the dinghy.

We worked at low water that evening and removed many more things, until the ship was free of obstructions below. That night we forsook the lean-to for a small cave under an overhanging cliff, where we built a fire and were quite comfortable in our sleeping bags. Although the situtation was bad, we had plenty of supplies for the time being, and it was midsummer.

The next day dawned clear and cold, but warmed up as the sun rose. We extracted the last supplies from the boat by swimming for them, and I finally found the catsup for which I had been pining. After a hearty meal we were leisurely cleaning the salt water out of our gear, guns, sextant, glasses, etc., with blankets and clothing spread out to dry, when we heard a gunshot from seaward. We could see nothing, but fired our guns in answer. Another shot followed, and soon we saw three kayaks coming toward us from the bay entrance. Then two more. The first three came to the camp and the other two turned off to the wreck.

They were very friendly, these Eskimos, or Greenlanders as those of mixed blood are called, and it was clear that we would get on well with them. We all gathered about the wreck, and there we all went to work. No words were spoken between us, but we demonstrated, with our knives, how we wanted the mainsail un-

24

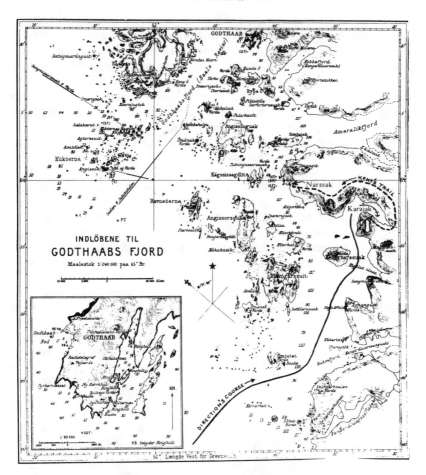

Chart of Karajak Fjord,
showing DIRECTION'S course
into the anchorage, and
Kent's overland trek
to Narssak for help.

bent, and in no time the crowd was at work, laughing and talking among themselves. Soon all sails and running rigging were ashore.

More kayaks arrived. The manner in which the natives handle these boats is beautiful. The kayak is a perfect thing, a development of this hardy race, and nothing could be better suited for their needs. The men, brought up to these little boats virtually from birth, handle them as if they were part of the body. They are very fast boats, quick and versatile, and cannot be swamped.

Since it was hot, we took a swim in the bay when we returned to camp. None of the Greenlanders know how to swim. But they enjoyed the show and staged one in return. Two of the most skilled hands with the kayak dressed in the waterproof jackets and hoods which are attached to the cockpit and rolled the boats over and over from a position at rest on the water. This is a remarkable feat of skill, requiring much practice. It is easy to turn over, but very difficult to continue around and up again, using the paddle as a flipper. This trick is used in seal fishing and in meeting large seas bottom-on.

More Greenlanders arrived in kayaks, and a boatload of children. The camp was overrun with them, and their laughter and talking

The next day, after the storm. The Governor of Greenland, and one of the Greenlanders in his kayak, examine the wreck in preparation for the salvage operation.

raised our spirits. Then one arrived with a letter from Kent who had arrived at the settlement, Narssak, and had sent a kayak to Godthaab for help. These Greenlanders were from Narssak.

The Governor at Godthaab received the message and proceeded at once to Narssak, accompanied by the local Governor and the doctor. There are two governors at Godthaab, a super-governor of Southern Greenland, and the governor of Godthaab itself. They started at once for the wreck in three powerboats, picked up Kent along the way and arrived at our camp late that afternoon.

We were introduced all around, and the men from Godthaab surveyed the wreck. The prospect of salvaging was considered, and then all retired to an anchorage off the camp. The Super-Governor invited us aboard his boat for supper, and we shaved and washed up for the occasion. After supper we looked over the wreck again, and it was decided to try and float *Direction* at high water, take all the gear aboard the Godthaab boats, and to proceed thence, towing the wreck.

The Greenlanders helped us collect the gear, while the Godthaab boatmen arranged 12 casks which they had brought to float the hull. Eight casks were put below and four were lashed outboard

En route to Godthaab.

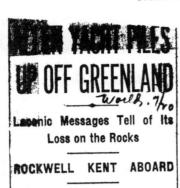

IN YACHT PILES

UP OFF GREENLAND

World, 7/10

Laconic Messages Tell of Its
Loss on the Rocks

ROCKWELL KENT ABOARD

Father of 22-Year-Old Skipper
Thinks Fog to Blame

COPENHAGEN, Denmark, July 19 (A. P.)—The American yacht Direction, in which Rockwell Kent and two young companions have been exploring the North, was wrecked last Sunday near Godthaab, Greenland, according to a telegram to-day from that settlement. The three were safe, but the yacht was a total loss.

Allen's Yacht
Piles on Rocks;
Explorers Safe

Herald - Tribune 7/10

Rockwell Kent and Companions Rescued After Crash Near Coast of Greenland

By The Associated Press
COPENHAGEN, Denmark, July 19.
—The American yacht Direction, in which Rockwell Kent, American artist, and two young companions have been exploring the North, was wrecked last Sunday near Godthaab, Greenland, according to a telegram today from that settlement. The crew was saved, but the yacht was demolished.

"Safe and Well," Allen Wires

A cablegram from Arthur S. Allen Jr., youthful skipper of the Direction, to his father, who lives in Phillipse Manor, Tarrytown, read: "Lost ship on rocks—we are safe and well." Beyond this message, and a garbled cable from

at her bilge, bow and stern. High water, which covered her deck, came with early morning, and we canted her over the other way, from starboard to port, with a line from her hounds to one of the powerboats. In the meanwhile, all of the gear had been loaded from the shore, and as the water neared peak flood all three boats got lines to the hull to pull her off.

There was some difficulty in starting her off the rock shelf; it required much pulling and hauling. The outstanding note of the whole procedure was the competence and ability of the Greenlanders at their work. They marked themselves as sailors. It is natural to them—seamanship is part of their lives. So she came off, as a result of their forethought and action more than of ours, and we proceeded out the bay for Godthaab. *Direction* floated at her deck line, and if any of the casks had sprung, she would have sunk as we towed her. With the three boats towing ahead we made a curious sight as we proceeded at 1.5 knots. It was a dreary scene to me, but it was great to see her free again.

Our crew of three were aboard the Super-Governor's boat, with the two Governors and the doctor. Coffee was served from time to time, and we talked. There was food, too, including *paté de foie gras*—not quite in line with the fare one usually associates with shipwrecked mariners. In "Camp Direction" we enjoyed squab, and now *paté*!

We were all very sleepy on the passage. The oil engines pounded on, the quiet, efficient Greenlander engineers watched over them, and we dozed on the settees. But at length we reached Godthaab, and the Super-Governor's boat cast off the tow and went alongside the dock, while the rest came to anchor. The whole town was out to see us, more than 100 people at the pierhead. We must have looked rather tough, but they seemed to like us.

The doctor took charge of Kent, while Cary and I were whisked away in tow of Governor Simon of Godthaab, who took us to his house immediately, where we were greeted by his wife and shown to our rooms. Hot water was ready for us and we had a real wash, with clean towels. Then the Governor took us to the store to pick out clothing. We chose some blue pants, socks, underwear and fine cloth from which were made the beautiful jerkins and hoods which all Greenlanders wear. These latter required but a few hours to make. Then back to the Governor's house for a wonderful dinner! Afterward we went to the storehouse to check up on our gear which had been brought ashore.

That afternoon the Greenlanders began work to haul *Direction* out of the water on a long incline of round timbers laid close together longitudinally, which was built for that purpose. Here again, the wonderful skill and vigor in the work these men do was evident. They produced fine gear, a coil of two-inch rope, a tremendous set of falls, jacks, a windlass and a big oil engine. She came up enough so that she was clear in low water, and we all had a good look at her in the evening. Kent and Cary, with many others, spent some time inside, giving things away—the few remaining medical supplies to the doctor, toys to the children, etc.— while I surveyed the damage from outside and tried to decide about repairs.

She had three major holes to starboard, all below the water line, one about six feet by three, and the other two about two by three feet across. She was badly beaten up, but it is remarkable how well she had stood up. She was not, I think, badly wracked and strained in other parts than those holed. Her heavy construction had stood her in good stead. A block of about 30 or 40 pounds was gone from the forward end of her iron keel, and her stern was badly mashed astern of that, but the scarf, stern and keel were

not started, and neither member was broken. Her keel was also chewed at the stern, the wood part abaft the iron ballast being knocked out, and the heel of her rudder had worn away. The rudder hangings were all solid. They were of fine workmanship. A knee had been so heavily pushed at the top of her bad hole amidships that it had raised her deck planking a bit at one spot, but this was not badly broken.

Except where she was in direct and irresistibly crushing contact with the rocks, she did not seem strained or marked at all. For a while I sat on the beach and considered starting immediately to put in new pieces of frames and replank those holes, so as to sail her back as soon as we finished—in late August, I hoped. But since lumber was not available, and there were no power-driven tools, it appeared that it would be impossible to float her and fit her out for a return to New York that summer.

After surveying the wreck, the Governor showed us the town. It is a pleasant, happy place, larger than we expected, and carefully laid out. The oldest houses are turf huts with wooden framing, very interesting; but most of the houses are of wood. The governor's house, where we stayed, is the most elaborate in God-

thaab. It is of stone, 200 years old, the oldest building in the town, and the best built. All the explorers have lived there at various periods—Nansen, Rasmussen, MacMillan, Peary. It is beautifully appointed, with fine furniture, a large library of valuable books, many paintings and a general atmosphere of comfort.

We sent messages home and gathered in the living room for the evening. The Governor produced cigars, vermouth and a fine bottle of whiskey. Then to bed, and a good sleep.

Next morning we found that *Direction* had been hauled clear of the water and lay in an absolutely safe place. A conversation with the Super-Governor revealed that the repair work was out of our hands. Both Governors were making reports to Denmark, and the Danish Government, which is in charge of all work done at Godthaab, would take charge of the repairs. There was one good shipwright in town, who was very busy, but he would start at once, working a little each day, and the boat would be ready next year, when I could come and get her.

This was, of course, the best of news, and we began to think about plans for getting home. So far it had been impossible for us to pay for any of the hospitality we had received, and we felt

31

a little awkward about it. There was a chance of getting a steamer from Ivigtut, at the southern end of Greenland, within a month, bound for Philadelphia. There was also a steamer which would call at Godthaab in a few days bound for Denmark with a stop at Ivigtut. The only way to get to Ivigtut is by boat, as the land is impassable in any direction.

So we decided to collect, check over, list and store all gear and leave the ship to be repaired during the winter; and to come back the next year, fit out, and sail over to Denmark, where we would ask for an audience with the King, tell him we liked his people, and thank him kindly.

Kent decided to stay in Godthaab a while, taking a later ship for Denmark. This he did, bringing home with him many paintings, this being the object of his part of the adventure.

The following day we went to the home of the Super-Governor to make formal declaration of the wreck—and it was formal! The Governor, in epaulets and a sword, led us to the courtroom, where we were seated at a council table with the two Governors, their assistants and an interpreter. We gave our account of the wreck and signified our intention of having the ship repaired there. This would require cabling for a set of plans to be sent to Denmark. these to be sent on to Godthaab with the materials. The cost of salvage, i.e., kerosene, labor, etc., would be paid by the government, according to their custom. The actual cost of repairing the ship I arranged to pay.

It was arranged that we were to sail on the freight steamer which would arrive in Godthaab the next day and leave four or five days later. After the session in the Governor's chamber we retired to the living room for tea served by the Governor's wife.

During the next few days, while we were waiting for the ship to leave, we were royally entertained, not only by the Governor, but by many of the other townspeople, who were very cordial.

Our steamer arrived during the night, July 21, and was to sail July 25. She was *Brattinsborg*, 1100 tons—a tramp steamer. We arranged for two bunks in the fo'c'sle and were to eat in officers' mess, all for six *kronen*—$1.50—a day! She had a cargo of 72,000 bottles of beer for Ivigtut and would stay there about 12 days, taking on a cargo of cryolite for Denmark. The passage to Copenhagen would take about two weeks. Many of the crew spoke some English, and the officers were fine men.

Before we left we made a trip to Narssak to get some things taken from the wreck and to pay the Eskimos who had helped us.

We were given a warm welcome there, too, and recovered more blocks, spars and some of Kent's canvas.

As the time for departure drew near, we completed our packing and the storage of the ship's gear. We had been able to buy some beautiful things from the Eskimos, and had arranged to have others made for us during the winter. We paid our farewell respects to Super-Governor Petersen, who showed us the letter in which he had begged the Danish government to grant us permission to return next year and wished us all good luck. The morning we sailed I went over *Direction* with the carpenter, a fisherman serving as interpreter, and made a list of the materials to be ordered in Denmark. I decided to replank the whole starboard side in view of the cheapness of labor and the fact that the job would be better. I felt confident that this work would be well done by the Greenlanders. The doctor's boat, as big as ours, had been even more damaged the year before, they said, and is as good as new today.

Then we took our leave of all the fine people of Godthaab. We waved goodbye again and again from the ship, until Godthaab was out of sight.

The next day we reached Ivigtut, after running into fog and passing some large bergs. By the time we reached the settlement, we were many miles inland. The town itself is a surprising sight for one who comes to Greenland because it is a primitive place. It is a mining town, producing cryolite, a mineral used in making the famous Copenhagen china. The captain took hours to moor the ship, with anchor, chain and stern line, to a large buoy off the quay, and five times to shore. They take great pains in mooring here because of the storm winds off the mountains.

Ivigtut Harbor and wharf, Greenland.

33

During the 12 days we spent in Ivigtut we explored the mine thoroughly, met many of the workers, and were entertained several times at the Director's house.

We sailed again August 7, and then began a long, lazy passage, one day much like another. We were comfortable aboard. The officers were fine to us, the meals good and frequent; we had American cigarettes, American magazines and American music by radio from London restaurants. We also had the privileges of the bridge, and the weather was beautiful, with following winds, S.W and W. What a time to cross the North Atlantic with *Direction!*

Our course left Iceland about 100 miles to port. Ten days out of Ivigtut we made a landfall, passing between Scotland and the Shetlands, and saw several steam trawlers. In the North Sea we had a taste of bad weather with some head winds and rain. The swells were short and irregular, not at all like those of the North Atlantic.

The last day of the voyage was marvelous. We were running up the Skagerrak before half a gale of clean, clear wind and blue sea flecked with much spindrift. The sun was bright and warm in the lee of a deckhouse or boat as we approached the Skaw, from which we would lay our course to Copenhagen. The visibility was fine, and there were many lights and day beacons.

Copenhagen tomorrow. The cruise was becoming very long—in mileage—but I was learning a great deal. I could not see a square mile of these waters without thinking how fine it would be with *Direction.*

We docked at Copenhagen on a lovely morning and arose early to see the beautiful north coast as we approached the city. We had a week in Copenhagen and enjoyed the time immensely, meeting everywhere the same Scandinavian cordiality, although our Greenlander clothes were looked at a bit askance.

On August 29 I sailed for New York via Oslo, Norway, leaving Cary in Denmark. He planned to return home by way of the Continent. I waved goodbye to him with much feeling as he stood on the pier in his dirty green *anorak.* He had stood up like a million dollars on this summer's work.

I was interested in the harbour at Oslo, where I saw many fine Norwegian double-enders. And so, to New York, with a quiet passage, on the whole, though we were under reduced speed from Halifax because of a pea soup fog.

We docked with the adventure all over.

34

STARBOARD TACK
By
Alfred F. Loomis
(1932)

AUTHOR'S NOTE: The adventures of Direction *and her crew were being covered by the press and particularly by* Yachting *magazine which was then under the editorship of Herbert L. Stone.*

After the death of his son, Arthur S. Allen Sr. decided that repairs to Direction *should continue, and that she should be brought back to Baddeck. The logistics of such an undertaking were formidable. Using lumber shipped from Denmark, a crew of Greenlanders repaired her under the watchful eye of the Greenland* Styrelse, *the Danish governing body for all Greenland. The* Styrelse *then arranged for her to be sailed 300 miles down the coast to Ivigtut, and there loaded on a steamer bound for Philadelphia.*

In New York, Herbert Stone arranged for Alfred F. Loomis to sail Direction *back to Baddeck.*

During the winter of 1945-6 when I was negotiating by telephone for the purchase of Direction, *I phoned Alfred Loomis, and told him of my plans, explaining that I understood he had sailed* Direction *from Philadelphia to Baddeck, Nova Scotia.*

"No," he said, "I took her as far as Cold Spring Harbor on Long Island, and that was enough for me." His reply was emphatic.

I told him that Direction *was at Pinaud's yard in Baddeck, that Pinaud had made extensive alterations to her and had told me she was in good condition.*

"Walter Pinaud built Hotspur *for me," said Alf, "and if he says* Direction *is okay you have nothing further to worry about."*

So I purchased Direction *on faith, without ever seeing her. My thought was that if she proved unseaworthy I'd simply spend my vacation on the Bras d'Or Lakes and leave her there.*

Here is Alf's account (from Yachting, *January 1932) of the delivery trip that led him to conclude that "Philadelphia to Cold Spring Harbor was enough for me!"*

A day of haze and lazy southerly swells, of sun and calm, as bubbles flowed past our dirty sides. A position off the Jersey shore beyond the line of lightships and unfrequented by coastwise vessels. And a Coast Guard cutter, a little ship of lovely yachty lines, roaming up under one engine to inspect us. My prejudices being what they are (this being in the days of Prohibition—*Ed.*), I had never thought to see loveliness in a rum-chaser, but there was beauty in this new motorship.

The chaser's crew came on deck to look us over, and what they saw would have brought the least interested to the rail—a gray, smeared hull, starboard sheer woefully hogged at the chainplates; a mast cut in a primeval forest, stayed (as if it needed staying) by four shrouds to a side and three forestays; a suit of stretched and stained tan sails, drooping listlessly in the calm, and a once-white spinnaker occasionally filling. We had only two marks of unmistakable artistry—name boards lettered by a master hand.

An officer stepped to a wing of the bridge and shouted a seven-word question which eloquently revealed the impression we had made upon him.

"Do you want us to report you?"

Had we sailed, perhaps, from Tasmania? Were we rendered desperate by these last days of September heat and calm? Were we overdue, with relatives ashore anxiously awaiting word of us? These things might have been, if our picture of dirt and hardship had cut true. But I replied, "No, thank you," and the Coast Guard vessel lazed off to westward.

The fact was that we were the cutter yacht *Direction*, two drifting days out of Philadelphia. She had previously sailed in the icy waters of Greenland, where she had been wrecked, and now, having been repaired and shipped to Philadelphia by steamer, she was bound for a Long Island port. Rockwell Kent, who lettered her name boards and cut in their feathered arrows, wrote splendidly of her in his book *N by E*. Arthur S. Allen Jr. owned and sailed her to an almost landlocked anchorage near Godthaab, where a gale swept down from glacial mountains and thrust her on the rocks. Then Allen, by the sardonic fate which seems to pursue fearless sailors, was killed near his home by a speeding motor car, as his beloved ship lay weathering ashore in Greenland.

She stayed there two years until Arthur Allen Sr. had her repaired and brought home. Home she was, or nearly so, when I reported aboard in the Delaware River to sail her to New York.

As my recent experience in sailing has been in a windward worker, she challenged me. I wanted to see how she would point, how she would sail, and how she would stand up in a breeze of wind—while I prayed for a fair slant between Philadelphia and New York. Mr. Allen is the kind of man for whom people do things willingly and gladly, but I lay no claim to a spirit of altruism in volunteering my services. I wanted to see *Direction* at work.

This famous cutter arrived at Philadephia on September 2 and was towed to the Kensington shipyard, three miles up river. I don't know how many years it is since this yard had harbored a sailboat, and a yacht at that, but there are men there who know and love a windjammer. How they worked! Many of *Direction's* furnishings had been sucked out of her by greedy breakers in the Greenland harbor, and in the repair work the starboard side of her interior had been removed. Lockers gone and bulkheads missing, bunks and chart table gone. Shipmate stove in place to port but rusted beyond use; port water tank stove in, but starboard tank intact. Lamps, binnacle and even her anchors bent and battered. Running rigging and lanyards for her shrouds weathered far beyond the point of safety. Decks dirty and interior filthy.

But by the time I reached her on September 8 she was livable and sailable. Her running rigging and her lanyards were newly rove off, her lamps were filled with oil; a new stove replaced the old one; bunks and mattresses were in the final stages of manufacture; and paint brightened her deck and cabin. Mr. Allen

DIRECTION docked in Philadelphia.

37

DIRECTION sailing during her trials in the Tappan Zee (Hudson River), New York, spring 1929. Note her angle of keel and how little wind is blowing. (This tenderness was the cause of Alf Loomis' strong criticism.)

bought a dinghy, portable icebox, blankets and galley utensils; a grocer delivered canned and fresh stores. At 3:00 on September 9, riggers, carpenters, and officers of the yard left her as a tug came up to tow *Direction* down the narrow reaches of the river.

I admit that I was aghast when I saw how this 33-foot cutter was built and rigged. Her beam is 11 feet—one in three—and our new 9½-foot dinghy stowed as comfortably between bulwarks forward of the mast as if it had been built to order. Her bowsprit is sheathed with metal, secured beneath with two half-inch chain bobstays, and against side whip by double half-inch wire stays. The mast is a solid spar, nine inches in diameter at the deck and not more than 36 feet tall. The shrouds, three to a side leading from the hounds, are of ⅝-inch wire, with topmast shrouds and backstays of only slightly less diameter. The forestay is heavier than any, and there is a jibstay and flying jibstay as well. To set up the rigging, tarred Italian hemp of 1¼-inch circumference reeves through four-inch deadeyes. Any item of this standing

38

gear would be suitable for a 70-footer, and any single shroud or stay would support *Direction's* gargantuan mast until the hinges of hell blew off.

Running rigging. I had never thought to sail with running parts that were hemp throughout—but so *Direction* is rigged: sheets, halyards, topping lift and backstay runners. The main throat and peak halyards and the jumbo halyards, as well as the mainsheet, are of two-inch stuff, but the mainsheet blocks are sheaved for still larger rope. I love hemp for its strength, and once my hands are toughened I don't mind the feel of it; but when it is wet and stiff and kinky I don't want to be shipmates with it.

Direction's hull is double-ended, and her keel, with 9000 pounds of iron on it, is long and straight. I don't know the siding and molding of her ribs, but they are proportionate to the other dimensions. They had to be heavy to withstand crunching on those rocks in Greenland. If a boat has a destiny (as I believe), this massive hull was built to be wrecked. By which I mean that no boat less strongly planked and timbered could have resisted the pounding of those northern seas. She invited it. And yet there is also bulk without strength. Bilge stringers and sheer clamps of heavy oak are butted end to end without scarfing.

Yet, again, here was *Direction,* survivor of an experience that would have splintered frailer craft, hardly leaking 10 gallons a day, and once more ready for sea.

I had arranged with my brother-in-law, Joe Burge, who is not a sailor, and with one other, who is superbly one, to ship with me, and had asked them to report aboard at 3:00. Before the hour Joe showed up, but where was the other man?

A call to New York located him at his desk. He was tremendously sorry, but he had "clean forgotten" his promise, and anyway he was too busy. I called Findlay Downs, rear commodore of the Corinthian Yacht Club of Philadelphia, and he promised to find us the necessary third man, and asked me and Joe to be his guests for the night at the clubhouse in Essington. I thanked him and accepted—for there are mosquitoes over the Delaware—and returned to *Direction.*

"We'll shove off," said I, "but I'll take no chances with a strange boat, so we'll tow the ten miles to Essington." Our motor tug drew six feet. I mention this unimpressive fact for the reason that if she had drawn less than *Direction* we would have parted her towline on Horseshoe Shoal, while if she had drawn more, we would have poked our bowsprit through the rear window of her pilothouse. But, both vessels drawing the same, we grounded together and, luckily, both bumped clear without damage. With a fair tide and no other incident, the tug delivered us to Essington at 5:30 and left us to the mercies of the mosquitoes.

Joe and I remained aboard only long enough for a change of clothes and then went ashore in the Corinthian's club launch. The rear commodore was there to greet us, and two friends of his took us up to a room where in the wicked era *(before* Prohibition—*Ed.)* an oak table used to feel the delicate caress of whisky glasses. Ho hum, the good old days!

We were late to dinner, but not too late to interview Pete Christianson who took a chance and signed on for our voyage. Pete's last yacht had been sold beneath his feet, as it were, and he was temporarily out of a job—so I took advantage of his adversity to inform him that while under way he would cook, whether or not he could.

There may possibly be more hospitable clubs than the Philadelphia Corinthian, but I have never before arisen after a night spent dreamlessly beneath mosquito bar to be informed that the club launch would tow us to that point at which the wind would fill our sails on an easy reach. Such was our good fortune, and against a flood tide we were towed 20 miles to New Castle, Delaware, where a gentle southwesterly rippled Delaware Bay. We took on stores at New Castle—for Pete, being an ex-deepwater man, is a great believer in bread and potatoes—and then, just below the town, we raised sail and let go the towline. God knows how many days the tow had saved us. Though *Direction* has no motor, we were now independent.

In laying out this cruise I had allotted, roughly, two days for the jaunt down Delaware Bay, two for a reach across to the end of Long Island, and one for a run up Long Island Sound to Cold Spring Harbor. But I did keep other wind conditions in mind and, before bidding Mr. Allen goodbye, I had informed him that if we were headed when halfway to Montauk Point, I would run for Ambrose Channel and enter Long Island Sound via New York Harbor. That, I told him, would mean an expensive tow through Hell Gate, which I hoped to avoid by going east-about.

As we let go our towline I saw no evidence of the hard wind that I hoped would blow us down the river and eastward to Montauk Point. I was more than a little surprised to see, however, that as we fell away on the starboard tack we took a very sharp heel.

"I thought she'd be a stiff boat," said Pete, "and here her rail's almost under."

"It's the stores and stove on her port side," said I, "and don't forget the weight of her mast and rigging. Also the gaff."

We looked at the gaff, a ponderous stick, almost untapered, and concluded that it was at least twice too heavy.

"I guess," said Pete, "she's one of them bruisers that lays down just so far at a breath of air and don't go beyond that."

"Here's hoping."

We had a favoring tide by this time and, although the breeze momentarily went light, we made fair time for three hours. To weather Stony Point Shoal we had to sail her pretty close-hauled. I was amazed to see by bearings on the shore how far the boat was sagging off to leeward.

Pete remarked, "Looks like she's one of them two-way boats— makes as much leeway as headway."

But the current eased us around the curve in the river and we eased sheets for the reach down Liston range. After that the tide turned and the wind faded more. In the first four hours of the night we progressed only four miles. Even this was better than anchoring, and the business of sailing kept one of us on deck to entice the mosquitoes away from the sleeping watch below. The ebb of the tide brought strength to the wind, and morning saw us off Brandywine Shoal, still on the starboard tack. For six hours we held our own while the current surged up the entrance to the Delaware. After that we passed over the tip of the Overfalls, confident that the now outgoing stream would keep us off the shallow spots shoreward. At 3:00 in the afternoon, off McCries Shoal buoy, I figured that we had come 50 miles in our first 24 hours of sailing. Put down 10 miles of that as preponderance of ebb over flood tide, and 20 more to the use of the spinnaker; the remainder was all *Direction's* working sails had been able to wrest from the light southwesterly.

By this time, with plenty of sea room and a surprisingly quick grasp of steering by compass, Joe was able to stand a watch alone, and the night passed quickly. Not so *Direction*. In the morning we were not much more than 10 miles beyond Northeast End Lightship, and I had begun to think that a course for the New York Harbor entrance would be advisable.

The Coast Guard cutter mentioned earlier looked us over just before a new slant of wind came in from the northeast. We took in the spinnaker and after a try at sailing *Direction* close-hauled and a glance astern at our wake, my change in plans crystallized. We started sheets on a course of N by W for Sandy Hook.

That was quite a pleasant little breeze of 10 knots. Surprisingly, our rail went under often enough to fill a bucket that had been lashed in the lee rigging. I wondered how much stiffer she would be on the port tack, but we never left the starboard.

What's a day more or less? Sunday noon, four days out of Kensington, saw us drifting aimlessly across Gedney Channel in New York's lower harbor. The northeasterly had been succeeded by a southerly calm and in the last of the slack we unlashed the oars from the cabinhouse and rowed out of the channel to find an anchorage.

I had made my plans, and as plans should be, they were flexible. If there was a little wind at the turn of the tide we would drift in to Gravesend Bay and anchor. Then Joe and I would go by train to Cold Spring Harbor and return with my own boat to tow *Direction* through the harbor. But if there was a little wind, we would carry on to an anchorage off New York's East 26th Street. If there was a strong fair wind and we had also a fair tide, we would sail through Hell Gate. This last seemed a remote possibility.

A wind came in at 3:00 and I awoke from a nap to find Pete getting the anchor aboard and *Direction* making faint headway against the tide. Momentarily the wind strengthened from south-southeast and by the time we had set the spinnaker (again to starboard) we were doing better than a mile an hour over the ground. Pete wanted to unmake the port anchor but I told him to leave it ready for instant use, and to have the 20-fathom hemp hawser clear for running.

*Deck view of DIRECTION
taken from the hounds
by Alf Loomis.*

42

DIRECTION'S massive standing rigging. The 5/8-inch shrouds, seized instead of spliced, are still at Pinaud's yard in Baddeck. One of the deadeyes decorates the author's mantel, while the two sheet blocks are still in use half a century later.

We dodged across Ambrose Channel between bellowing steamers, and on the chart I ticked off the buoys as they passed. At Number 12 we sighted, close aboard in the fog, a yawl under power and a motorboat, seemingly directionless. Some minutes later they faded away, off our starboard beam.

At buoy 14 we jibed over—our first and only adventure on the port tack. Soon the flood tide caught us, and just beyond, the fog scaled off. The wind hauled to south of west and I commenced to feel exhilarated. Once before I had sailed a boat that would not go to windward and on that occasion, in 2000 miles of cruising, the wind had nearly always been abaft the beam. And here was *Direction*, four days underway, sailing on one tack, never close-hauled, and now with the wind obligingly shifting as our course changed. Who said there are any perils in Hell Gate?

We passed through Buttermilk Channel. Entering the East River, the first eddy caught us as we passed beneath Brooklyn Bridge. The sudden reversal of our ship's head should have warned me. Instead, as I slacked off the main sheet and jibed around, I felt a sense of mastery. We were on our course again, sweeping slowly up river, and there was just enough wind in the puffs to give us steerageway. Where the river swept over to the Wallabout Basin I edged in to the New York side, and when we came abreast of the 26th Street station of the New York Yacht Club I renounced all thought of anchoring. The current carried us on, and of the wind, once more fair, I asked nothing more than steerageway.

43

Pete, crouching beside me, warned of the tide dividing on the rocks off Welfare Island, but I had been watching the flashing light and told him that we would clear it nicely. So we did. I gave Pete the tiller and turned my torch on the chart spread out on deck beside me. When I took over again, 15 seconds later, *Direction* was out of control. It was not Pete's fault. Able sailor though he is, he does not control the winds, and the southerly chose our shift of helmsmen as its moment to die away.

In the darkness I reached for the tiller and found it hard aport. I hauled the mainsail flat, and Joe let go the headsail sheets. Futile. The tide had taken control and was driving us toward the projecting New York piers. Pete moved forward quickly with one of our eight-foot oars to paddle our bow around. Joe picked up the other and backed water on our starboard quarter. The tiller still aport, I sat, fascinated by our approach to the pier.

Slowly our bow swung to starboard, and we missed a collision by a few yards.

"Got by that one," I called to Pete. "Don't pull her around any more."

But the next instant another swirl of the tide set us toward another pier. Pete rowed frantically and saved us from crashing bowsprit-on. We struck square on the port bow, and the rebound bounced us clear. As Joe hauled in the mainsail to keep the boom from swiping the bollards on the pier, a drunk standing there whom it just missed called out, "If yer do that here, watcha gonna do in Hell Gate?"

There was a question for you.

I had not thought of anchoring, for what could an anchor do when one is barging into piers? But as we caromed clear, a whirlpool caught us, turned us completely around and started us around again. For the moment our headlong movement was all but stopped and, as our bow swung upstream for the second time I shouted to Pete, "Let go that anchor, quick!"

Luckily for us the hawser was clear for running. Pete paid out the cable, all but 20 feet of it before the hook caught on the rocky bottom. Just abreast of us I saw the colored lights of the Montauk Yacht Club's 52nd Street station, and below them an immense, substantial float.

"She's holding," said Pete, "but I'd better let go the heavy anchor."

"I'll get the key," said I, for the key had been hurriedly made in Philadelphia, was a tight fit, was not galvanized, and I had put it below to keep it from rusting in place. Pete is a fast worker. When I reached him with the key, he had chain out on deck and was ready.

"The damned thing won't fit," said he.

"It will," I contradicted. "I've already tried it in the slot."

"It won't fit when the anchor is made up."

"Use wire."

"I've got a sail stop—" and Pete lashed the stock in place across the shank. While he did that I looked ashore again.

"Don't anchor," I said. "If I put the tiller hard aport we'll veer right into the float." I leaped aft and swung the tiller over.

"A heaving line," said Pete, coming aft, and I yanked a coil out of the lazarette. "It's that same goddamned hemp," said Pete, but heaved it nevertheless. By this time we were only 15 feet from the yacht club float. Men standing there caught the line. Small as it was it would have held us, but it fouled and there was no time to make it fast. Pete and Joe had to drop our end.

Out into the stream we charged again. But I had to wait until *Direction* swung before she responded to the ported tiller. Then we went in again, faster than I had yet seen the hooker move, and would have struck the float if the dragging anchor had not let us swing below it. The heaving line came flying back to us again and this time Pete made it fast. In water that was almost slack we moved upstream and then lay securely beside the float.

So we towed through Hell Gate on the morning tide, and filled our sails on the starboard tack near Execution Light and sailed peacefully down Long Island Sound. As we turned into Cold Spring Harbour, I remarked that there was almost always a southerly coming out of the harbour and that for once in our voyage of five days we would have to tack. But after a few feints from the south the wind held true in the west and we reached right in to our anchorage.

We doused the two jibs and with slack forestaysail and mainsail sheets I swung the cutter into the wind, telling Pete not to anchor until we had gathered sternway. But, heading west, I couldn't find the wind's eye.

"Where the devil is it?" I called to Pete.

"South," said he. "Just shifted."

"Then let go anyway."

I went forward to watch the chain pay out. Pete looked up, grinning.

"If the owner ever wants to rename this packet," said he, "he could call her *Starboard Tack*."

A POSTSCRIPT TO "STARBOARD TACK"

AUTHOR'S NOTE: In 1933 my good friend Al Stanford sent tear sheets of the above Loomis article to Rockwell Kent. Al was at that time editor of the Colophon, *a rather erudite publication of the graphic arts and Kent was a frequent contributor to the magazine. Kent replied as follows:*

March 16, 1933

Alfred Stanford Esq.
36 Orange Street
Brooklyn, New York

Dear Mr. Stanford,

Thank you very much for sending me that fine article from *Yachting.* I have read it with great pleasure and, I may say, felt some satisfaction in Mr. Loomis's vindication of my secret knowledge that the *Direction* was a cumbersome and topheavy craft, calculated to give its crew as rough an experience at sea as anything that ever sailed. His comment about the size of the gaff amused me because that great log and the spars in general were things that I picked on before the boat was even launched. I don't know much about boat construction, but I have had a good deal of experience as a carpenter and a pretty good sense, I think, of the engineering of all construction. I dislike surplus bulk even more than I fear weakness. There was another little detail of the boat that I picked on for criticism when the boat was being built, that was the cumbersome boom crutch; I said it would break. It did.

That was a beautifully written story of Mr. Loomis's.

Sincerely yours,

Rockwell Kent.

(Photo on next page):

Joseph A. "Red Rory" MacLean, at the helm of BABA last of a long line of ferry boats operating between Lower Washabuckt and the County seat of Baddeck. For more than 145 years five generations of MacLeans have carried the mails on the government-subsidized run. BABA was ketch rigged, the sails backing up a Gray Marine motor. In earlier days oars and sculls served the same purpose for scows that could carry a horse-and-buggy for the 1¼-mile run. It was Mr. MacLean who retained the DIRECTION logbook kept by Edward L. Ayres until my eventual visit.

Joseph (Red Rory) MacLean

THE AYRES LOG:
From Long Island to Nova Scotia
(1932)

*AUTHOR'S NOTE: Margaret and I were total strangers to Washa-
buckt, Cape Breton Island, when we arrived there with* Direction
*in 1966, so it came as a pleasant surprise to have Joseph A. "Red
Rory" MacLean accost us in the general store and tell us that he
had recognized* Direction *two days before as we sailed into the
Bras d'Or Lakes. After speaking to us, Joe went home and within
the hour had returned with the log (as mentioned in the preface to
this book) that had been kept by Edward L. Ayres when he delivered* Direction *to Baddeck in 1932. Arthur Allen Sr.'s summer*

47

studio was on the lake, and when he died in 1945 it was Joe MacLean's job to clean it out. Being a sailor, he recognized the worth of the logbook and saved it from the rubbish heap.

I had met Edward L. Ayres in 1948. He greeted me one day when Direction *was lying at the wharf in Essex, Connecticut. He made a brief visit aboard, during which he told me of his passage to Baddeck, also arranged by Herbert L. Stone, on the final leg of* Direction's *long homeward trek from Greenland.*

It's interesting to consider just what faced the man who sailed her home. Here was a boat without power, with top-heavy rigging, that had been wrecked, and then repaired by the Danish Government with absolutely nobody in charge who could be expected to take a personal interest from the point of view of a yachtsman. How Alf Loomis ever got her to Cold Spring Harbor is a wonder. How Edward L. Ayres got her to Baddeck I shall try to explain with a shortened version of his log, as follows:

Direction and her crew departed from Cold Spring Harbor, Long Island, at 9:00 P.M. on July 22, 1932. By 4:00 A.M. on July 23 they were off Middle Ground Lighthouse in very light winds, carrying their spinnaker. They made good time for such conditions and were opposite Horton's Point Lighthouse 13 hours later. Here Mr. Ayres began complaining in the log: "Boat needs ballast. Too tender." (*Since then I have added 2,000 pounds of lead in her bilges.*) By midnight they were becalmed in The Race, but at 2:00 A.M. July 24 they picked up a brisk northwest wind so that they entered the channel leading to the Cape Cod Canal at 6:00 P.M. Ayres noted a compass deviation of 14 degrees east on a course of northeast—not a very comforting bit of information.

They were towed through the Canal at 9:30 P.M. and departed from the Canal sea buoy on the north end at 11:00 P.M., on a course for Marblehead. The following noon, July 25, they were only off Plymouth but were able to set their spinnaker again, in a southeast breeze. Here Ayres notes that "the taffrail log is no good. The spinner is too small and the log chatters." They dropped anchor off the Eastern Yacht Club, Marblehead, Massachusetts, at 6:00 P.M., Ayres noting: "Tanks make a racket. Don't believe they have baffle plates. Afraid they may burst." (*New tanks with baffles were installed in 1945, and again in 1960.*)

The morning of July 26, in Marblehead Harbor, Ayres made note that they had taken on water and supplies, tried to buy a bilge pump without success, and had no workable taffrail log.

48

DIRECTION in the Bay of Islands, Newfoundland. Robert Hartwell Moore was in the process of overtaking DIRECTION when he shot this 1937 photograph; in 3 hours, DIRECTION had gone from being a dot on the horizon ahead to a dot on the horizon astern.

"11:30, weighed anchor." They took their departure from Thatcher's Island for Cape Sable, Nova Scotia, at 2:15 P.M. Ayres wrote: "Boat sails at large angle of heel. Think should have more ballast and a gallows frame." (I installed the gallows frame in the late 1950's.) For the next four days they saw no land but were able to get sights of Polaris, Vega and Mars. They had to estimate their speed and distance run, and on July 27 bailed 85 pails of water out of the bilges. (Remember, no bilge pump.) By the next day they had run into the usual Nova Scotia fog so got no more sights. That day they bailed only 50 pails of water, and Ayres noted wistfully: "Wish we had a pump."

The entry for 1:30 A.M. of the morning of July 29 reads: "Hear Sambro Light Vessel. This puts our DR track 3 miles to east. A steamer passed close astern of us headed NNE, and nearly ran us down. We lit flares and she altered course. Very foggy. Set clock ahead to meridian 60."

There was, of course, no electricity on Direction so her lights were all kerosene-burning and dim. Beginning at 6:15 P.M. that day there are several entries of interest: "Fog all day, no fix for two days. Sun peeped through this morning. Took some sights but all uncertain. DR position puts us off Whitehead Light, Cape Canso WSW ¼ W, 30 miles. But who knows(?) Wish we had a log."

"6:45 P.M. Hove to under jumbo and double-reefed mainsail to wait for clearing of fog. Course SE. Heaves to very comfortably. Will steer herself in a steady wind."

"9:30 P.M. to 11:00 SSW squalls and rain. Blew hard. She needs ballast! Deck leaks around the mast."

"5:00 A.M. July 30. FOG. FOG. FOG. Still hove-to, waiting for this fog to lift. Leeway ½ knot, perhaps offset by current. Cannot see ⅛ mile. Too risky to run in on the land. This is *EXASPERATING!* We were quite sure of our DR last evening but didn't dare risk the rocks off Canso. *(This was where* Shanghai *was wrecked in 1924.)* Nice SW breeze. There should be a seacock on the sink outlet. When on a starboard tack, water slops up over sink." *(We installed a seacock in 1958.)*

"7:45 A.M. Fog has lifted slightly. Shall we run in?"

"8:15 A.M. Clear. Took sights."

"8:45 A.M. Under way—plain sail NE X E compass NE ½ E?"

"9:00 to 11:00. Sun gave us sights. First fix in 2½ days. Must be strong set as our offing was greater than expected. Position, long. 61°-45', lat. 43°-30', steering course to Cape Canso light NE ¼ E. Allowing nothing for current which is supposed to set SW and 3 deg. west deviation. Wind SW, speed 4 knots."

As they approached their destination, Mr. Ayres made notations for Mr. Allen's benefit, but none of the recommendations were carried out until I owned *Direction* 15 years later. In an entry for July 30 he wrote:

"The boat has a decided list to port. Compass has a marked deviation. Port bearing cap on the windlass is cracked *(It still was in 1977!).* She leaks about 25 to 30 buckets per day, needs baffle plates in the water tanks, needs ballast. Needs seacock on sink outlet. Gallows frame would be handy. Log is worn and spinner not right size. Pipe or spigot for water tanks allows little water to come through. Needs outboard vents for tanks." *(Installed in 1945.)*

They picked up the Cranberry Island Lighthouse off Canso in the early hours of July 31, their sixth day at sea, (ninth day from Cold Spring Harbor), passed through St. Peters Canal and locks at 1:15 P.M. August 1, the following day. By 6:30 that evening they were at anchor in Baddeck. What a cruise!

DIRECTION as we first saw
her at Pinaud's wharf in 1946.
Virginia Ladd in the foreground and
Alexander Killam Murphy by the mast.

DIRECTION HEADS HOME
(1947)

AUTHOR'S NOTE: I wrote the following article for Yachting in
1947; it is the fifth episode in the continuing saga of Direction.

World War II had come to a close. There was a wild scramble to
get out of uniform and back into mufti. Nobody ever spoke of
"wooden boats" since wooden boats, the only kind available, were
taken for granted. Ocean racing was still a "gentleman's" sport
and yachtsmen were so few that yacht clubs were actually looking
for new members, and isolated harbors were still just that.

Gesture won the Bermuda race of 1946. Alexander Killam
Murphy had declined an invitation to sail as a crew member
aboard her, and instead made the cruise with us from Baddeck to
Connecticut aboard Direction, mostly because my invitation had
included his wife. The CCA Rule reigned supreme although already some grumbling was heard about violation of its spirit. The
I.O.R. Rule had not been thought of. My article on this cruise,
with my wife, Margaret's, illustrations, arrived late at Yachting's
editorial office but they ran it promptly as being "timely" for the
forthcoming resurrection of the Marblehead-Halifax race of 1947.

51

To buy a boat sight unseen is always risky. But if that boat is also 1000 miles away and you have only a two weeks' vacation in which to sail her home, then you are really asking for trouble. Nevertheless, that was what I committed myself to do in the summer of 1946. In the light of day I could face the undertaking with equanimity, but I had a habit of waking in the night and thinking about it while cold shivers ran up my spine. The decision was made, however, and, come what might, the cutter *Direction* was waiting in Nova Scotia for me to sail her back to Connecticut.

Our cruise really started from our home in New Haven at 4:00 A.M. on July 4, 1946. There were six of us in the car, on the roof were nine duffel bags, in the trunk was a deflated, five-man rubber lifeboat plus coils of manila from my old boat, a Lothrop foghorn, a sextant, a chronometer, a ship's clock, a barometer, a nautical almanac, charts, a Primus stove and countless other minor items that, by telephone calls and letters to Nova Scotia, we had determined were needed. It is interesting to note that, in spite of *Direction* being fully found, we still had a carload of gear to take to her.

Three days and two nights on the road, driving from dawn to dusk, brought us to Baddeck. There, the first thing we saw was *Direction* lying at Walter Pinaud's wharf. We had no need to ask the way: We spotted her from a quarter mile off and drove directly to her. That moment of climbing aboard was the climax of six months' planning and anticipation. We clambered excitedly all over her, absorbing as many details as we could. For six months I had been trying to visualize what she really would be like. Would I find her to be all that I had hoped for?

Also, I had been eager to meet the owner of the voice I had grown to know so well over the long-distance phone from Baddeck, the voice that had inspired me with such confidence in this undertaking. I was not disappointed in my meeting with Walter Pinaud. He had taken possession of *Direction* as she lay in his yard after the death of Arthur Allen Sr. a year before, and had fixed her up for his own use. This included the installation of a wartime surplus Jeep engine, a 3KW gasoline generator, a new 40-foot hollow mast with a Marconi mainsail.

Now he had her in such shape that we could have sailed away that very afternoon had we so wished. Only those who have experienced frustration in shipyards can appreciate what a miracle that was. In fact, Mr. Pinaud prides himself on having boats ready for their owners to the last pinch of salt or can of beans, so that

they may step right aboard and be on their way. In our case, however, we planned to do our own provisioning.

We arrived late Saturday afternoon and spent the rest of the day
settling on board. Our crew consisted of three couples: Alexander
K. Murphy and his wife, Shirley; Mynart Ladd and his wife, Virginia; my wife, Margaret, and myself. "Marty" Ladd was to be
our navigator, and the women divided the galley chores; otherwise, we had no special assignments except our regular watches.

On Sunday we were off for a shakedown cruise to Boulaceet
Harbour, the "Hamburg Cove" of the Bras d'Or Lakes. Cape
Breton Island is the northeasternmost extremity of Nova Scotia
from which it is separated by the Gut of Canso. In the center of
the island are the Bras d'Or Lakes, famous for their scenic beauty.
They are accessible from the north by the Great Bras d'Or and
the Little Bras d'Or, two channels which empty into Cabot Strait.
To the south, at St. Peters, there is a canal and lock leading to the
Atlantic.

The estate of Alexander Graham Bell is at Baddeck, and we
sailed by it as we started out for Boulaceet. We had plenty of
wind that day, which was a good thing for revealing any weak
spots in our craft. We soon found that our jibtopsail sheets were
rotten as we parted first one and then the other, and had to douse
the sail in quick order. Otherwise everything seemed shipshape.

Boulaceet is a small V-shaped cove with a shale bar extending
three quarters of the way across the mouth, giving completely
landlocked protection. Here we anchored for the night after a
brisk sail down the lake. Next morning we powered back to
Baddeck to buy food and attend to other last-minute chores.

We would have been happy to spend the entire summer just exploring the Bras d'Or Lakes, but we had a long cruise ahead of us
and our time was short. Our plan was to keep going steadily,
stopping only for supplies, to use the engine whenever needed,
and to lose no time being sporty by beating to windward against
light headwinds.

Roughly, we had 300 miles of Nova Scotian coast ahead of us,
200 miles of offshore sailing across the Gulf of Maine to Cape
Cod, and then another 100 or so miles to Essex on the Connecticut
River. (By the time we got home, we had logged 750 nautical
miles, while our car speedometer had registered 1049 statute miles
driving to Baddeck.)

The Nova Scotian coast has a rocky, indented shoreline with
many outlying dangers. The harbors are such a distance from the

shipping lanes that you lose half a day getting into one. Lighted whistling buoys, known as "automatics," lie about eight miles offshore and about 12 miles apart. We planned to sail from one of these to the next, right down the coast. Farther offshore lie the terminal moraines of the great glacier known as "The Banks," one part of which, rising above sea level, forms treacherous Sable Island. Other parts of the same moraine system form Georges Bank, Nantucket, Cape Cod, Block Island, and even Long Island. Georges Bank, with a least depth of three fathoms over Cultivator Shoal, must be avoided because of the steep seas which build up over it. As it lay directly in our path, we would have to pass either to the north or south of it. All these factors had been pondered over during the winter months as we studied the charts which occupied every available bit of wall space at home.

We were treated royally in Baddeck. Everyone knew *Direction* and seemed sorry to see her leave. The ration board gave us four weeks' supply of ration tickets apiece (in case we were becalmed), and we were able to stock up with food such as we had not seen throughout the war.

By Monday night we were ready to sail. So, after a good night's sleep, we were up early Tuesday morning and on our way. Walter Pinaud seemed sad at our departure. I think he felt as much attachment to *Direction* as I do. "Well, it's only right that she should go back to the States," he remarked.

We powered through the lakes in light airs and, before entering St. Peters Canal, swung ship for compass deviation. Marty Ladd superintended this job and, thanks to his painstaking skill, we managed to come out right on the nose on all of our courses thereafter. It turned out we had a 13° compass error, so it was well we checked.

We were through the locks at St. Peters by 5:00 in the afternoon, scratching our heads over the problem of identifying the Nova Scotian aides to navigation. Spar buoys look like little sticks floating in the water. Can buoys lie on their sides and appear more like steel drums with rounded bottoms; nuns are cone-shaped right down to the water line. It took us quite a time to get used to them and made us realize what a big part flash recognition plays in our lives without our being aware of it.

Then, of all lucky breaks, we got a northeast breeze. Quickly we hoisted sail and turned off the engine to find that close-hauled we could easily fetch Cape Ronde on Madame Island, and weather the dangers off Cape Canso. As we passed Green Island, we could

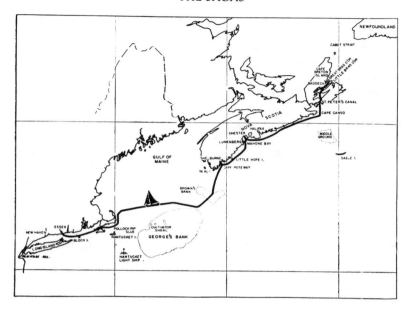

see enormous breakers two miles to windward offshore on Or-
pheus Rocks. We shuddered at the sight of them and vowed to
keep close track of our dead reckoning. This is no coast to approach when not certain of your position! The buoys are so far
apart that you can make a landfall without necessarily sighting
one, and could easily come to grief on some outlying reef. However, when you do find a whistler in a pea soup fog, it is a great
comfort to see neatly lettered on it the name of the harbor off
which it is situated.

Our northeast wind held and by dark we had rounded Cape
Canso and squared away before the breeze. Shirley Murphy and
I had the 8:00 to 12:00 watch and, about 11 o'clock, we noticed the
lights of a vessel dead ahead. We altered our course a bit as she
seemed not to be under way and we thought she might be fishing.
The vessel then moved and came to a stop, again directly in our
path. We started to trim in again to weather her when we heard
shouting and realized that we were being hailed. She was a large
diesel-powered fishing boat with a nest of dories showing in the
after cockpit under the glare of her deck lights. What were those
lights on shore? they wanted to know. They were just in from
Middle Ground near Sable Island and were not sure of their posi-

55

tion. Shirley called through the megaphone that the white flashing light was Cranberry Island. I wonder if those fishermen ever before had a woman help them out in their navigation! With a "Thank you, we're all set now," they started up their engines and headed eastward.

Psychologists tell us that man is happiest when he is successfully approaching some given objective. My crew shared with me all through this trip that exuberance that comes only at rare moments in life when some such objective is being attained. Whereas for many people the war years had meant a broadening of experience, we had found it quite the opposite, with our horizons constantly diminishing as we concentrated on the task at hand and failed to partake of any even slightly glamorous undertaking. Now here we were suddenly set free—doing things that seemed utterly remote from our everyday life. When Margaret and Alexander came on deck at midnight that first night to relieve Shirley and me, I had no desire to turn in, much as I knew I should.

This cruise in reality consisted of three separate cruises of three separate watches. Each individual saw at best only two thirds of the coast. One third of the time he was asleep and another third found him off watch attending chores below or otherwise not having an eye on the horizon. Since none of my crew were talkative we rarely knew what had been going on when we were off watch except for reading brief notes in the logbook.

There is something about the routine in a boat that makes the time pass quickly. It is hard to remember what events take place on what day, or even keep track of the days themselves as they speed by. Our first day we logged 82 miles, half under power, half under sail. The second day, all under power, we logged 117 miles. It was somewhere along here that Ginny Ladd produced a baked ham complete with cloves from the oven of our little Lunenburg stove. And, to our amazement and delectation, at another meal a crisp, brown prune souffle appeared. How Ginny did it in all that sea and motion I'm sure I don't know, but it added greatly to the crew's morale. Upon going off watch at midnight Wednesday, we had Sambro Light Vessel, off Halifax, nearly abeam.

In the small hours of the next morning, I was awakened by the wail of our fog siren to find that we were approaching Mahone Bay in a flat calm and heavy fog. Thanks to Marty's careful piloting on his watch, we picked up Northeast Shoal whistling buoy right on the nose, and then poked our way blind into Mahone Bay. We got fleeting glimpses of East Ironbound Island and Little Tancook Island, and then the fog shut in so we could hardly see 50 feet ahead.

One loses perspective in a fog. When Shirley spotted land, I thought I saw distant bluffs with green hills behind. Actually, the hills were trees 100 feet ahead and the bluffs were boulders. A glance overside revealed bottom right underneath us. The lead showed three fathoms, and we guessed our land was Woody Island, near Chester. We circled the island, keeping the bottom just in sight. We could hear someone hammering away at carpentry quite close but could see nothing. A fisherman finally verified that our landfall was indeed Woody Island, so with renewed confidence, we poked our way slowly to the town dock at Chester.

Our purpose in coming so far off our track was to combine a little sightseeing with the need to buy gasoline, but we found that in Nova Scotia if you want gas you must buy a 55-gallon drum of it. This is delivered by truck to the dock and then it is up to you to get it into your tanks. We heard there was a gas pump at Lunenburg so we decided to go there.

We had not been at the town dock at Chester long before we were welcomed by a couple who introduced themselves as the Daniel Blains. They were cruising people themselves, they explained, and knew what yachtsmen far from home needed most: Would we not care to come to their house for hot baths? We marched in shifts to their home with our towels slung over our shoulders. It turned out that the Blains were Americans who summered at Chester, and that we had friends in common back home.

Chester is a resort town with an American colony. It lies at the head of Mahone Bay which, when the fog burned off, revealed itself as a beautiful spot, dotted with islands of all sizes and descriptions. One of these is Oak Island, famous as the site of futile treasure excavations that have been going on since 1796, with more money being sunk in digging than will ever be recovered in doubloons. If anyone has met with success, it was never publicized. In the 1939 enterprise, air photos of the island were found to tally with charts known to have belonged to Captain William Kidd, so there is good reason to feel that he had some connection with it.

Another island in the bay is Tancook, birthplace of the Little Tancook schooners. Some of these schooners arrived at the dock later on that morning and they were a joy to behold. Though they are crudely built, they have a pleasing sheer and a well-traveled, seaworthy air about them.

At Chester we were introduced to the Canadian liquor laws. One can buy liquor at the liquor commission but may not consume it in public. Captain Hutt declined a drink when aboard *Direction* explaining that the law permitted him to drink only in his own boat, and then only if his boat were provided with living quarters. A pile of blankets in the forward cuddy served as proof that he was complying with the law as he drank his beer while rafted up to *Direction*.

That afternoon we sailed down the bay to Lunenburg with a brisk breeze, under a bright blue sky but with our fog bank still lying off the mouth of the bay. Lunenburg is the most important base for fishermen in Nova Scotia and is famous as the former home of the schooner *Bluenose*. Early the next morning some deep-water draggers came in from the Banks—huge, bald-headed, diesel-powered schooners with nests of dories on their decks. The fish are unloaded, placed on conveyors, and go through a regular production line with men in oilskins and boots cleaning, icing and crating them, while refrigerator cars wait at a siding.

Ginny Ladd made a trip to the Lunenburg Foundry, where our stove had been made, to get concentric ring lids to fit our various pots, and by noon we were ready to leave. No sooner were we out of the harbor than we dove right back into the fog bank. We ran under power in calm weather and thick fog from one automatic to the next. Rather than deviate from our course to pick up the Liverpool automatic, we made a beeline from La Have to Little Hope Island, a distance of 30 miles. We felt confident that if we missed the whistler off Little Hope we could hear the fog gun.

Shirley and I were again on the 8:00-to-midnight watch as we approached Little Hope Island. At intervals, we would turn off the motor and listen, then start up again for another 10 minutes of running. With Shirley up in the bow, her dripping oilies glistening in the glare of the 40-watt trouble lamp we had lashed to the forward side of the mast, I would stop the motor. "I heard something then," she would say, and I too would hear a distant boom, which we knew must be the gun going off at two-minute intervals at Little Hope Island. Then we would run the engine again while Shirley steered and I listened. Presently I could hear the gun without shutting off the engine. Before we realized it, we not only heard the gun but could feel its concussion in our eardrums and in the deck.

DIRECTION under power off the coast of Nova Scotia, approaching Little Hope Island with its fog gun booming. In 1946 this was one of the last guns to be used along the northeast coast. It was activated by acetylene gas and sparked by a timing mechanism.

"What's that strange roar?" Shirley asked as, with the motor off, we failed to have our accustomed silence. "Surf!" I answered. How close we were to that surf we shall never know, but I did not like it. Then, off in the distance, ever so faintly we could hear the groan of the automatic that lies offshore and beyond Little Hope. We were about a mile off our course, the only time on the whole trip that we did not fetch our mark within easy earshot. Shirley went forward, and when she felt that I had *Direction* headed for the buoy, she signaled, and I noted our compass course. We went on our way, leaving the roaring surf and booming gun of Little Hope astern with no regrets at parting company.

We continued to stop the engine at intervals to listen. Each time the whistling buoy sounded closer until at last a flashing red light loomed up through the fog, practically on board. We were so glad to see it that we circled it three times while I went below to lay our course for the next one. It was reassuring to read the words "Little Hope" on this buoy and "Lockeport" on the next one. This identification is so much more positive than the numbers we have on our U.S. buoys.

Margaret and Alexander were on watch by the time we passed Lockeport and headed for the Shelburne automatic. As daylight began to appear, we laid our course for Shelburne Harbour with Cape Roseway diaphone getting louder and louder off our port bow. We hove the lead on the way in, and our soundings jibed perfectly with our DR. Presently we sailed out of the fog into clear weather right on our course at the entrance to Shelburne. The fog still lay offshore, waiting, we presumed, for our return that afternoon to plague us through the tide rips off Seal Island.

At the head of the harbor we made fast to a wharf and went ashore to stretch our legs. I persuaded the driver of a gasoline truck to take me back to *Direction* where he tanked us up to capacity. With our two 15-gallon drums on deck, this gave us a cruising range of 240 miles, just about the distance from Shelburne to Chatham, Massachusetts. It eventually turned out that we were still using this gasoline on weekend cruises long after we got home.

At 11 o'clock, a brisk northwest breeze sprang up which quickly dissipated all fog, and we cast off from the wharf under forestaysail. Eagerly we set all canvas, including spinnaker, for a rollicking run under clear blue skies down the bay to Cape Roseway. Then, with spinnaker doused but still with started sheets, we headed out to sea on a course that would take us to the south of Georges Bank. We had in mind the prevailing southwest winds and felt that the more weatherly advantage we could gain for such future winds the better. If they failed to materialize, we could continue on this course, eventually fetching Nantucket Light Vessel, and then go home by way of Montauk Point, Long Island.

Now for the first time we were getting into regions where tides are an important factor. That night, we were sailing along at about two knots in a light breeze, supposedly out of sight of land. Shirley and I were listening to the voice of Van Deventer, coming to us from the WOR news room in New York on our portable radio, waiting for the weather report which followed at 11:30. I happened to look astern and noticed two flashing lights that had not been there a few moments before. A glance at the chart identified them as Blonde Rock and Seal Island. They were doing better than we were on our southwesterly course and threatened to overtake us! We ran the motor for a while until we put them comfortably below the horizon again. The strong flood tide had been setting us in toward the Bay of Fundy faster than we had been sailing through the water!

This was the first night that we had been able to hear Station WOR on our non-marine portable radio. We had hoped to be able to use the time tick to check our chronometer, but both Sydney and Halifax had stations giving time ticks so we had been all right. It was interesting to note each night as we crossed the Gulf of Maine how WOR became clearer and clearer. The familiar voices gave us a comfortable feeling of nearing home.

By evening of the next day we had crossed Browns Bank, and the wind had swung around to the south, so we altered our course to skirt the northern edge of Georges Bank. Marty was able to get star sights morning and evening, so we knew pretty well where we were.

Monday was overcast with a brisk wind from the northwest and we sailed at a good clip under forestaysail and double-reefed mainsail. It was the kind of day when those off watch lie in their bunks to keep from getting tossed about and no one feels like cooking hot meals—or eating them, for that matter.

Later that day we altered our course to cross that of a steam trawler, to check our position. "One hundred and forty-five miles east-southeast of Boston," was the skipper's reply. That put us about 13 miles east of our DR position. Shortly after, the sun came out and Marty dashed for the sextant. His line of position intersected our track about four miles west of our DR. That was good enough for us.

That night Alexander and I switched watches, and I was at the tiller with Margaret at about 2:30 A.M. The moon was shining brightly. Suddenly we saw, right abeam of us and less than 50 feet away, what looked like a rock awash. There was a noise of escaping air and a splash, and we realized that we had disturbed a whale. I was comforted by the thought of our 1½-inch planking and 2½" x 3" frames.

We were below at breakfast the following morning, with Alexander at the helm, when he jumped up and disappeared from our view over the cabin roof. "Land! I see land!" he shouted.

We all clambered on deck to behold Cape Cod standing out dimly but definitely on the distant horizon, with a tall tower to prove that it was no illusion.

We were still clad in our Nova Scotia cold-weather garb which, for me, consisted of heavy woolen underwear, woolen socks, woolen shirt, slacks, a sweater, a fleece-lined vest, and a slicker jacket. The others were similarly dressed when on deck. Within an hour I was stripped to the waist, wearing only shorts and sneakers—much more fitting dress for mid-July. Our Lunenburg stove had been burning steadily since we left Baddeck, consuming practically all of our supply of coke and firewood. Now we let it go out for the first time, and did our cooking on the Primus. I know of no other region where such a spectacular change in climate takes place as in the Gulf of Maine. I had experienced it before, going in the other direction, with the sensation of stepping from a warm room into a refrigerator.

It was 8:00 A.M. when Alexander sighted land. At 1:00 P.M. we were sailing in a fine southerly through Pollock Rip Slue into Nantucket Sound with a strong ebb tide paradoxically helping us on our way. The tide seemingly ebbs from the ocean *into* Nantucket Sound. Actually it is ebbing from the Gulf of Maine into the ocean *via* Nantucket and Vineyard Sounds.

We considered stopping somewhere for the night but, when the wind continued to hold, we decided to make the most of it and keep going. By 2:00 A.M. we were out of Vineyard Sound. Ten o'clock saw us at Champlin's dock, Block Island, where we telephoned our families and reported our arrival in home waters. Then we sailed on into the Sound, and up the Connecticut River to Essex, where we made fast to the Essex Paint & Marine Wharf in time to go ashore for a meal at the Griswold Inn, our first shore meal since leaving Baddeck 10 days earlier.

"That's all very well," you may say, "you got the boat home all right, but what happened to the car?" In the beginning of this story did I intimate that Walter Pinaud provided a unique yachting service? If not, I surely meant to. He topped it off by introducing us to Gordon Harrigan of Cape Breton Island, who at that moment wished to visit his sister in Connecticut. Thanks to him, our car was waiting for us when we got home. What more could anyone ask?

62

*Rose Blanche, typical of south
coast villages in Newfoundland,
lies at the eastern terminus of the
highway from Port aux Basques.*

A CRUISE TO THE SOUTH COAST OF
NEWFOUNDLAND
(1971)

AUTHOR'S NOTE: My next story about Direction *appeared in
the February 1971 issue of SAIL magazine. The cruise reported
took place in 1969, the first year of my retirement, several years
after* Direction *had been given a diesel engine, a ton of lead internal ballast, roller-furling jibs, a gallows frame—and other improvements to make her a more comfortable and seaworthy
cruising yacht.*

*This article makes quite a contrast to the log kept by Edward
L. Ayres and the other earlier accounts of* Direction's *sailing abilities which appear in this book. By this time* Direction *was 40
years old, and I had owned her for 23 years.*

*I should also remind you that with my retirement, and our pur-
chase of some land not far from Baddeck,* Direction *was sailed
back to Nova Scotia, and took up permanent residence there—in
summer on a mooring lying just off our property, and in winter,
hauled out at the Pinaud yard.*

Cabot Strait runs between Cape Breton, Nova Scotia, and the south coast of Newfoundland, and it can be a pretty cold and miserable place when the fog closes in—even during the middle of July.

"Anyone who cruises those waters must be out of his mind," says my good friend Al Stanford. He is right in some ways, of course, but if you share my own emotional approach, which defies logic, you will understand after you read this article why we like these waters.

There I was on the midnight-to-dawn watch, wearing Norwegian net underwear next to my skin, followed, in order, by a suit of quilted underwear, woolen shirt and pants, a mackinaw, and topped off with foul-weather gear and boots. And do I call that fun? Yes, damn it, I do—but don't ask me why!

Down the hatch, a coal fire glowed in our Lunenburg Fisherman stove. The kettle simmered, and the dim light over the chart table gave just enough illumination so I could see Margaret preparing a savory cup of beef bouillon to pass up to me on deck along with a handful of crackers.

Dave and Grace Bacon, the balance of our crew, slumbered peacefully below in the forward cabin. Visibility was a dank 100 feet horizontally, but from time to time a star would show through the thin layer overhead.

The wind had petered out an hour or so before and we were motoring. Our three headsails were rolled up on their Wyckham-Martin furling gears, and the main boom was securely sheeted down in the gallows frame.

The remains of a swell, further confused by unknown currents, tossed us enough to make Margaret mutter something about "getting too old for this sort of life."

No matter how much confidence you may acquire at home all winter, as you pore over charts and study the loran lines of position, when you are out there again, you always feel a certain apprehension. At least I do. Especially at a time when we are approaching the bleak and unfamiliar coast of Newfoundland at night in a fog, with only one line of position readable on our DX navigator.

The cathode-ray tube of our loran set glowed reassuringly when tuned to 1-H-1, with its master station on the eastern end of mainland Nova Scotia, and its slave at our destination near Port aux Basques. But do you think we could pick up *another* pair of signals to give us a second line, and a fix?

No such luck! And thanks to the late arrival, too, of the most recent "Canadian Notice to Mariners" we did not know of the change in frequency and signal of the RDF from Channel Head Lighthouse. The master signal of loran 1-H-2 came in sharp and clear, but evidently its slave at the opposite end of Nova Scotia was just too far away for us to receive.

The gods were with us that night. Just as we were reading the last line of position from 1-H-1 before closing the coast into the unreliable loran area, and being forced (heaven forbid!) to consult our trusty taffrail log, which we had trailed astern like a vestigial appendix, the stars came out!

The dawn appeared shortly thereafter, cerulean and gold, and what at first seemed to be our fog bank lurking in the distance materialized into Table Mountain—gorgeous, awe-inspiring, and

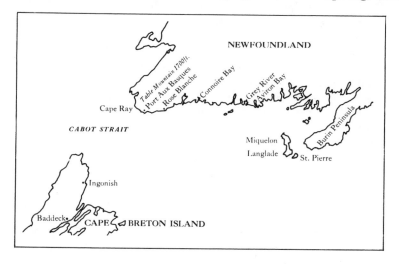

dwarfing the Cape Ray Lighthouse that stands on a low peninsula below it. This was living! This was our reward for the long night, all the cold, discomfort, fear and apprehension.

This was why we had sailed our cutter *Direction* from Essex, Connecticut, and kept her in Nova Scotia on the Bras d'Or Lakes, where easy access to such wonders could be had almost overnight.

We have based *Direction* at Pinaud's yard in Baddeck since 1966, and I sometimes wonder if we'll ever sail her back to crowded Long Island Sound. With the ultimate in cruising grounds lying at our very front door, it would be difficult ever to consider leaving.

We left Baddeck on a sunny morning in mid-July, and anchored that night under the mountains bordering the charming harbour of Ingonish on the northern peninsula of Cape Breton. We made a late departure the next morning to time our arrival off the coast of Newfoundland at dawn: If my navigation were faulty we'd have a full day to find a port. As it turned out, we were safely in Port aux Basques, Newfoundland, by 0730.

Our arrival marked an anniversary of sorts. Just 40 years earlier, in June 1929, *Direction* had first sailed into Port aux Basques with Rockwell Kent and his youthful companions. Ashore, I dispatched a letter to Kent telling him where the old boat was.

Port aux Basques was hustling that morning. Seagoing ferries ply between here and North Sydney, Nova Scotia, carrying American and Canadian tourists by the thousands. Word has obviously got around that here is an unspoiled wilderness right in the backyard of America and just awaiting exploitation. But it is safe for a while. Once east of Rose Blanche harbour on the south coast there are no more roads. Beyond here nothing has changed since the days of Jacques Cartier and John Cabot.

Boats still reign supreme all the way to the Burin Peninsula 130 miles to the east. Sailing and character go hand in hand in this part of the world. Which is cause and which is effect, I would not know, but I do know that anywhere you may go in the world (provided you can penetrate the language barrier) you will find in the sailor a kindred spirit. And in Newfoundland we are in a foreign land but with no language barrier!

Sam Mousseau was on his fishing boat that morning and saw us enter the harbour. After a day's work, he came over and gave us a hail. It never occurred to him not to, nor was he at all surprised when I immediately asked him aboard. Here was a boat that interested him. He knew boats and took it for granted that he would be welcome—as, of course, he was. This encounter with Sam was repeated many times down the coast. Getting to know people like him and obtaining, through them, a fleeting glimpse of a way of life that is vanishing from the earth is a reward that alone would have made our trip worthwhile.

In Port aux Basques, or to be exact, Channel, where the small boats dock and the village lies, we found *Corisande* and *Nima* awaiting us. *Corisande* is a yawl owned by Dr. Daniel Blain of Philadelphia, and hails from his summer home in Chester, Nova Scotia. Dr. Blain is the man who offered us hot baths back in 1946.

Nima is a 23-foot Pinaud-built sloop in which its owner, Captain John Parker, takes busman's holidays from his duties as superintendent of pilots for the harbour of Sydney, Nova Scotia.

The waterfalls at the Barasway in Harbour Le Cou invite exploration and topping off of water tanks.

All three craft flew the burgees of the Cruising Club of America. The Bras d'Or post ot the CCA had organized this week-long cruise and we represented three quarters of the expected fleet. The fourth quarter appeared the next morning exactly on the appointed hour. She was the famous yawl, *White Mist,* once campaigned and cruised in both the North and South Atlantic by the

67

*Billiard Cove, on Connoire Bay, Newfoundland, with NIMA,
CORISANDE and DIRECTION rafted up together. So
different from Grey River you would think you
were on another continent.*

late Blunt White, and now owned by our Bras d'Or post captain, Melville B. Grosvenor, whose exploits are well known to readers of the *National Geographic. White Mist* had just completed a most unusual six-week passage, and it was nothing short of remarkable to have her show up precisely at the appointed hour.

She had departed from Annapolis, Maryland, and rounded Cape May before sailing up the Hudson River. Her mast was removed to transit the Champlain Canal, then restepped to sail the length of Lake Champlain. The mast was again lowered for passage through the Richelieu Canal. It was restepped again, for the final time, for the sail down the St. Lawrence to Quebec, the Gaspé, the Magdalen Islands, and finally here, Channel, Newfoundland, where she arrived exactly on schedule.

For the next week, the four boats coasted to the east, anchoring in separate harbors on some nights and meeting, by prearrangement, on others. We were lucky with the weather, having blue skies and comfortable westerlies, which meant rollicking spinnaker runs for us on *Direction.*

One could spend a dozen summers on this coast and still find new and delightful spots to explore. There are fjords, inlets and harbors spaced only about five miles apart for more than 200 miles. The scenery is fantastic and, surprisingly, each fjord has an individuality, differing from its neighbor in some singular aspect.

Gray River, for instance, is entered by a narrow slot in a cliff. It would be nearly impossible to find were it not for the tiny light-house perched halfway up one rock face. A formidable tide rip greets you as you approach. And as you gaze in awe at what nature has concocted, the tiny village of Jert's Cove appears on your left. You may secure there for the night at a wharf, or continue for miles of sheltered waters that open out into lakelike spots of tranquil beauty.

But Connoire Bay is so different from Gray River you'd think you were on another continent. Here rolling hills allow moose to feed right at the water's edge. No forests, no cliffs, only lush green tundra-clad hills, subtly inviting you to hike on what actually is nearly impassable bog-like terrain.

Billiard Cove in Connoire Bay offers one of the most secure anchorages on this coast. Dave Bacon clamped his portable depth-sounder to the transom of our dinghy and guided us in. There is room for only one boat to anchor here, so the other three rafted alongside *Direction*.

Farther east is La Hune Bay with its vertical walls rising from 30 fathoms deep to an altitude of 1000 feet in one breathtaking swoop. Right around the corner lies Aviron Bay, a favorite of most who visit this coast. At the head of this fjord a fall of clear and potable water cascades down 300 feet of rock into a pool — a perfect spot to fill jerricans and top off our water tanks.

You would think you were at the end of the world in Aviron Bay, but actually right next door lies the charming village of François (pronounced Frans-Way), where adequate supplies may be had from the Penney Store. All you have to do is work your way out of Aviron Bay and turn left. Within a few miles or so you see a lighthouse perched about a quarter of the way up the cliff. Head in, and there you are.

From either Aviron Bay or François on a clear day the French island of Miquelon can be seen 30 miles off. We were lucky to have a daytime passage, with all of Miquelon standing out sharp and clear. It was early afternoon when we made St. Pierre, the only port in the islands. If you are looking for a foreign country, you don't have to bother to sail across the Atlantic when you

69

Grey River, 25 miles away from Billiard Cove, is entered through a narrow slot in the cliffs hidden from seaward. Here DIRECTION seems dwarfed by the grandeur of the anchorage.

have this charming bit of France lying within reach of a summer cruise. The adventure began when we closed the coast of Mique-lon, and met our first St. Pierre dory. These boats run to about 30 feet in length, and have a perky sheer with gaily painted top-sides. Then came our first French lighted-whistle-buoy which was fairly dripping with Gallic atmosphere. Once in the harbour, an official-looking man in a beret directed us to our berth at the customs wharf, and presto! There we were in France!

We spent a week in the inner basin or, to be more precise, the inner holding tank. We were moored three abreast off the town's central quay, and apart from a sewer spewing effluent around our water line, it was idyllic. Not everyone spoke English, per-haps, but everyone who bothered to make friends with us did.

Jean Reux, one of the harbor pilots, came aboard for coffee several times. Like Captain John Parker (who introduced us), he is also a yachtsman. He sent us a Christmas card some months later with a colored picture of his husky seagoing dragger, con-verted for pleasure cruising.

Jean Letiec was another visitor. He was pilot of the DC-3 that flies passenger runs to Sydney, and we were rafted up to his motor yacht, *Tony*. On foggy days he'd come below for coffee, con-stantly peering out our hatch in hopes of seeing a clearing in the weather. One evening he arrived by dragger, having landed his plane on the beach that connects the islands of Langlade and Miquelon: The air strip at St. Pierre was closed in tight but the beach was clear. His passengers thought it was a lark and enjoyed every minute of it.

Jean Pierre Andrieux, who was featured in one issue of the *National Geographic* as the agent for *White Mist* on one of her earlier visits to this area, was a frequent visitor, and showed us his collection of clippings reporting shipwrecks on the island of Miquelon over the previous 50 years. (Since this was written he has published a book on shipwrecks.) These were only a few of the friendly visitors who made us eager to return to these islands in the future.

Our little "fleet" disbanded at St. Pierre, with *Nima* and *White Mist* making a direct passage back to Cape Breton Island. *Cori-sande* could not carry her mainsail, having sprung her mast in a blow off Aviron Bay, so we became her escort, and harbor-hopped back the way we had come. This was no sacrifice for we well might have gone home in this fashion anyway, just to explore still more enticing fjords and harbours. I often think back

St. Pierre is a bit of France lying just off the North American continent. The perky, colorful dories are hauled out every night, each with its own primitive capstan and ways.

with wonder to the words spoken by Al Stanford: "Anyone who cruises in those waters must be out of his mind."

Maybe so, but any time water skiers, holding tanks, crowded anchorages and bustling marinas start to get you down to the point where you feel out of your mind, there's a great wide wonderful world of uncrowded cruising waiting for you on the south coast of Newfoundland.

PART II:
The People Involved

Colin Archer (1832-1921)

A VISIT TO THE HOME OF THE LATE
COLIN ARCHER
By Robert S. Carter
(1973)

AUTHOR'S NOTE: Boats are designed by people, built by people and sailed by people. It takes people to maintain them whether by paying the bills or by doing the work themselves. This obvious remark is not so obvious when you consider how many little people—unknown to the public—contribute their considerable skills to a finished product in which their part goes completely unrecognized. Many of these people are artists in their own right, who perform their special skills every day to earn a living, while those "at the top" receive the public's accolade. I have in mind the dot-etcher and engraver who produces the beautiful color illustration we admire so much in a magazine, or the "unknown" artisan who produced the lithographs from the drawings Rockwell Kent made on stone.

With that as a backdrop, as we sit in Direction's cozy cabin, let me now introduce to you those people most directly involved in the creation of Direction. Let's start with this article by my friend, Bob Carter.

Among the foremost pleasures of foreign cruising are the occasional and often fortuitous personal contacts with people of other cultures with whom we find a bond of common interest. When Carl Vilas asked me, while I was cruising Norway in 1973, to see if I could turn up any references to Colin Archer for him, I did not think it would lead to such a contact, although I was glad to try. I suppose I pictured a few minutes in the card file of the Bergen Public Library as my contribution.

But one thing leads to another, and the difficulty of using a Norwegian card index, plus an attractive English-speaking librarian, found me explaining my project to her, which in turn caused her to go digging for references in sources outside her library. This produced a list she had ready for me on my next visit to Bergen. And in turn this led to the suggestion that the library in Larvik might prove to be a richer source—Larvik being Archer's birthplace and hometown. (This solved the puzzle of whether he had been born a Scot or a Norwegian, on which there had been some difference of opinion: his parents had moved from Scotland to Norway shortly before his birth.) Larvik lies on the southeast coast of Norway and, as my wife and I were planning to put in for a visit to a nearby port two weeks later on our return to Sweden, stopping at Larvik was no problem. Our hostess there kindly lent us her car, and telephoned ahead to the library to explain in Norwegian our objective. So upon arrival at the Larvik library all its Colin Archer references were assembled.

While asking some questions at the desk, the librarian appealed to the next man in line for help in explanation and, on hearing my mission, he said, "Well, Colin Archer's grandson is my best friend. He lives just up the street in the old Archer house. Come along and we'll find him."

Soon we were sitting under the big trees on the sweeping lawn, looking down the Larvikfjord, and talking with the grandson, Lektor Justus Henry Archer, who is a physics teacher, plus a great grandson, who works as a computer technician, and a great, great granddaughter, who was at the moment changing her doll's diapers. Drinking tea on the lawn with the Victorian house standing behind us, its six generations of the Archer family in our minds, and carrying on quiet conversation, we were suddenly taken back to the ambiance of the 19th century.

A second personal contact came from another yachtsman, Mr. Jan Wilsgaard, chief designer for Volvo in Göthenburg, who owns two Colin Archer boats and is himself assembling a library on the subject. Some weeks later, on the evening before we sailed from Göthenburg for France, Mr. Wilsgaard found us at the boatyard. How different were the conditons of this second meeting. A storm wind was driving rain squalls across the evening sky, a young Swedish couple was having dinner on board with us (while their newborn baby slept in the forward cabin). All this while the boat was in the normal state of presailing disarray. We had to coax Mr. Wilsgaard to come aboard, but I was certainly not going to lose that last chance to complete my research for Carl, and I believe it resulted in a mutually profitable exchange of notes. Some of the references I had already found were new to Mr. Wilsgaard, and I was also able to suggest that he locate a copy of Billy Atkins' *Of Yachts and Men,* if he wanted to follow the development of Archer designs in the United States.

Since Carl Vilas had been looking for the source of transition of the *redningskoite* plans from Norwegian to American drawing boards, I must quote from the Atkin book that it was William Washburn Nutting who originally came across the Archer plans in a copy of Chatterton's *Fore And Aft Craft* which Carl Vilas mentions elsewhere in these pages. Nutting had seen and admired the *redningskoite Solapax* sufficiently to show a picture of her in his book *The Track of the Typhoon,* along with Claud Worth's famous *Tern.* But at that time Nutting was still sold on a hull like *Typhoon,* rigged as a schooner. Nutting also built a new schooner, *Harpoon,* but she became an uninsured wreck six weeks after she was launched, and was lying off Fort Totten, New York, where she was blown ashore in a gale.

By the following spring (1924), Nutting had purchased the *redningskoite Leiv Eriksson,* motivated in part by lack of funds and thus seeking a "bargain" in Norway. Most of my research for Carl has provided titles of books and articles unavailable in the U.S., but somehow he has been able to glean the information he wanted from the leads I was able to provide so my efforts have not been in vain.

*The COLIN ARCHER. Named after its designer,
this is the original* redningskoite, *photographed in Oslo, Norway about 1893. Photo
courtesy the REDNINGSKKELSKEPET, Oslo.*

COLIN ARCHER

COLIN ARCHER: Either you worship the name or you scorn it. If you are a cruising man who appreciates a solid deck under your feet, your heart may skip a beat at the sight of a double-ended Colin Archer *redningskoite,* swinging to an anchor in some remote harbour. Ranging in size from 28 feet to 47 feet, she may be gaff- or Marconi-rigged, a cutter, yawl or ketch, but she is always burdensome, broad of beam and exudes an atmosphere of seaworthiness that inspires confidence and admiration. If you are a racing man, your contempt for such a "monstrosity" may be only thinly concealed as you puzzle over the "taste" of some yachtsmen.

I know because in *Direction* I have owned such a vessel for more than three decades and have been fielding questions from sailors of both persuasions. True, there are neophites who have never heard the name "Colin Archer", or if they have, entertain only the vaguest notion of who he was and what his name stands for. If such is your case, you are not alone. Even the most sophisticated cruising veteran, if pinned down, will be hard put to be specific about Colin Archer. Oh, he may drop the name knowingly along with "Billy Atkin and "John G. Hanna", but if you probe for the source of his knowledge you will usually discover that it is mostly hearsay and legend.

A replica of a Norwegian NORDLAND boat, a type widely used until the late 1800s. This six-oared model was making a 500-mile voyage to Oslo, Norway, when photographed by Robert S. Carter in 1973.

There's good reason for this. Colin Archer's fame derives from the boats he designed nearly a century ago, of which one named *Fram* probably is the best known. *Fram* carried Fridtjof Nansen and Otto Sverdrup north to the Arctic icepack in the 1890's in a three-year attempt to reach the North Pole, and is now enshrined in a Norwegian museum. But for the yachtsman, Archer's pilot boats and *redningskoites* are of greater importance. The articles he wrote for naval architecture and sporting magazines between 1870 and 1900 contributed to his fame and legend, but most have since become lost in improperly indexed library files, or were simply thrown away. A nephew of Archer's has written a book entitled *Colin Archer, A Memoir,* which received limited circulation in Norway and England, but it is impossible to find the book in any university or public library in the United States. Still, Archer's legend continues to orbit the yachting world by word of mouth with no visible sources of input.

Norsk Selskab til Skibbrudnes Redning. What a mouthful for an English speaking yachtsman! According to Colin Archer's nephew, that title translates to "Norwegian Society for the Rescue of the Shipwrecked." Thanks to that organization and its secretary, Mr. Leif R. Lund, I finally found a copy of *Colin Archer, A Memoir* by James Archer, printed by John Bellows, Ltd., Gloucester, England. For all I know, it may be the only copy on this side of the Atlantic. It is written in English, all 120 Xeroxed pages of it. So, from here on, I speak with documented authority.

The Norwegian Society for the Rescue of the Shipwrecked was founded in 1891, and patterned after the much older English National Institution for the Preservation of the Shipwrecked, known today in England as the Royal National Lifeboat Institution. The original English lifeboats, however, were primarily surfboats, designed to be dragged across beaches and launched through the surf, and rowed to the site of a wreck. Norway, having no beaches, had to have deep-draft, sea-keeping craft that were decked over and propelled by sail rather than oars. Colin Archer was one of the founders of the Norwegian society, and designed its first boat, which he called a *redningskoite* (rescue boat) to distinguish it from the English lifeboat.

By 1891, when the Norwegian society was organized, Colin Archer's reputation was already well-established. He had perfected and revolutionized the local pilot boats by introducing carvel construction (in place of lapstrake), iron keels, deep draft and full decks, all of which were lacking in the open boats that Norwegian pilots were using when Archer arrived there in the 1860's. The pointed stern, most outstanding feature of the Colin Archer type, was a direct inheritance from Viking days. Today there are claims and counterclaims as to its merits. "Too little buoyancy aft," complain modern designers, "which exposes the boat to being pooped when running."

"Not so," say its exponents, "the pointed stern reacts kindly to a following sea and permits lying-to with a stern drogue." The *Colin Archer,* the prototype on which all subsequent *redningskoites* were based, was launched in 1893, and promptly sailed to the Lofoten Islands to take up station there with the fishing fleet. As of 1977, this vessel is still afloat, and in commisssion as a Sea Scout training vessel! She has survived 82 years of service.

Eventually, some 27 *redningskoites* were built and stationed in strategic places along the Norwegian coast. The perils of that coast are quite different from those of England or the United States. While the pilots of southern Norway had been persuaded of the wisdom of using decked-over vessels, fishermen still worked from open boats, especially an eight-oared lapstrake type known as the "Nordland." There was good reason for this. In the days before the internal combustion engine, you rowed or sailed to the fishing grounds, just as your Viking ancestors did for over 1000 years. You cannot row from a decked-over vessel, and fishing is much more convenient in an open boat where your hands are at a level with your jigs and trawls.

SOLVAER, the twelfth redningskoite built, was constructed in 1897, and continued in service as a rescue boat until 1938. These vessels were used all along the Norwegian coast, in the open ocean, and deep in the fjords, wherever seamen were in peril from great storms.

In Norway, above the Arctic Circle, there was a tremendous toll of lives each year in the open Nordland boats which depended upon human muscle and a square sail for power.

But the new *redningskoite* could go to sea, carry sail, and perform rescues in any kind of weather. She could pluck these imperiled fishermen from their helpless craft, provide shelter and safety, and sometimes salvage their boats as well. The very first mission for *Colin Archer* was documented, and provides a vivid picture of the sea conditions she could face and still bring off breathtaking rescues.

The fishing villages of Hamningberg and Vardo lie on the northeast coast of Norway facing the Barents Sea. They are 150 miles east of the North Cape, opposite Spitsbergen, Novaya Zemlya, and the Russian coast. They are 250 miles north of the Arctic Circle at 71° north latitude—the land of the midnight sun. On May 20, 1894, one month short of the summer solstice, in perpetual daylight, a gale of hurricane force, with driving snow, hit the coast. Since it was a Sunday, the fishing fleet was in harbor. Vardo had a breakwater that provided protection from the onshore northeaster, and the boats were in no danger. But in Hamningberg, 20 miles away, things became grim as great seas thundered into the unprotected harbour.

Most of the smaller boats had been hauled ashore but there were larger craft, with crews aboard, in danger of dragging their anchors or parting their cables. The *Colin Archer* was lying safely at Vardo when a telegram from Hamningberg arrived, asking for help. She and a steam-driven bait boat put out to sea after other steam-powered vessels in the harbor had declined to help. The bait boat had only gone a short distance before she was forced to turn back. The *Colin Archer* kept plugging on.

Let us turn now to the words of her master, Captain Anthonisen, for a first-person description of how it was that day:

K A P T .   N .   M .   A N T H O N I S E N

« C O L I N   A R C H E R »

"The snowstorm was so thick that we had great difficulty in keeping our course. The distance at which the land was visible was never more than one eighth of a mile, and sometimes only a few ship's lengths. We had started out at 5:30 in the morning and at about 8:30 we sighted Hamningberg. The sea was extraordinarily heavy. We stood down towards the breakers, going as near as possible. The entrance to the harbor was practically one great breaker. From here we could make out the boats and vessels lying in the harbor."

"Finally we went in and, by backing, filling, tacking and jibing as seemed best, in the course of three quarters of an hour we were able to take on board twenty-two souls, one of them a lady. They were ordered below, and we sailed out past the worst of the breakers and hove to. We dared not lie to farther in since we had our vessel so full of people. We waited and searched for any further signals of distress from other vessels in the harbour. Seeing none, after fifteen minutes we headed back for Vardo.

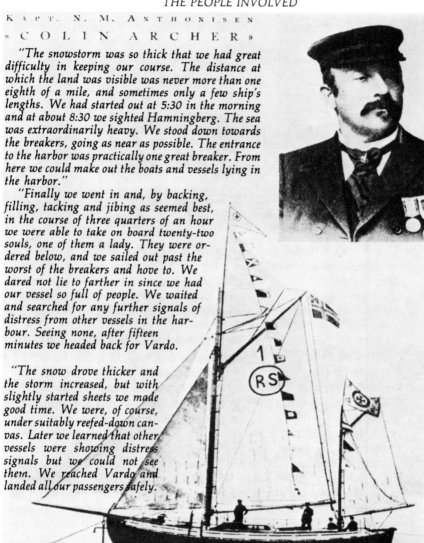

"The snow drove thicker and the storm increased, but with slightly started sheets we made good time. We were, of course, under suitably reefed-down canvas. Later we learned that other vessels were showing distress signals but we could not see them. We reached Vardo and landed all our passengers safely.

*COLIN ARCHER
as she appeared
in 1942.*

That was not the end for skipper Anthonisen. He returned to Hamningberg a second time, took off 14 more people, and landed them safely at Vardo. His risks were validated several hours later when several of the boats in Hamningberg were blown ashore and broken up on the rocks—where rescue would have been impossible.

Colin Archer must have been a sociable person. He was the first to introduce the sport of yachting to Norway in 1873. In 1883 he was one of the founders of the *Kongelig Norsk Seilforening,* the Royal Norwegian Yacht Club. In its official history, published in 1933, he appears in many group photographs and the book contains pictures of him and the yachts he owned down through the years, including smaller versions of the *redningskoites.* He served as commodore of the club in 1900.

Archer's writings influenced naval architecture for many years. His now-discredited Wave Form Theory was widely accepted in his day, and was applied by other naval architects in the design of commercial vessels as well as yachts. The lines of the *redningskoites* conformed to the theory, and here is how Archer described it:

"When a vessel is propelled through the water, it is found that the water is forced out of her way or a like quantity rises above the surface of repose and forms a wave or waves which assume a particular shape. If the vessel's entrance is of an unsuitable shape, and if she is propelled with considerable force, the water is displaced in a form which is not that of a natural wave. It will then, after a time, (besides the principle wave of displacement) break up into a series of smaller residual waves. These residual waves may be looked upon as representing the force wasted. We may therefore infer that the most suitable form of entrance is one which displaces the water in such a way that a wave of natural form will be [created] at every stage of its formation, and will at the same time absorb all the water displaced, so that no residual waves will be thrown off."

So far so good. But in later years, when Archer's theories were used to determine the areas of transverse sections of a vessel, and their rate of increase from bow to midship, his work came into conflict with later work in ship design.

Archer's father was a timber merchant from the Firth of Tay in Scotland. During the hard times and depression that followed th Napoleonic Wars he moved his family to an enchanting fjord in Norway. So, in 1819 he settled in Larvik at the head of Larvik Fjord, which faces Sweden across the Skagerrak, and is not far from the entrance to Oslo Fjord.

It was at Larvik that Colin Archer was born in 1832, and where Archer settled down in 1860, after years of wandering—gold-prospecting in California, coffee-growing in the Hawaiian Islands, and sheep-raising in Australia. He married a Norwegian girl, and his descendants to this day occupy his Victorian home at Tolderodden, on the outskirts of Larvik. Here he started a small shipyard capable of turning out his pilot boats and *redningskoites*. A few miles farther down the fjord he had a larger shipyard where he built the *Fram* and many other commercial vessels.

COLIN ARCHER
*as she appeared
in 1975.*

From *FORE AND AFT* by E. Keble Chatterton:
"In this illustration will be seen a photograph of a modern pilot-craft, which, except for being cutter rigged and for her internal fittings, is very similar to the redningskoite. She carries a large staysail and a small jib like the Bristol Channel pilot-craft. Like the latter, too, she is a staunch, plucky little vessel, having about 38 to 40 feet in length overall. Her mainsail is peaked very high, and she sets a small topsail. But it is her hull which is of such interest to us with its retention of those eminently northern features of which we have spoken already. There are several yachts in England of varying size which have been based on these pilot-craft, and if not fast in light winds they have proved themselves to be splendid sea-boats."

Among the many authorities with whom Colin Archer corresponded at the height of his career was the British author E. Keble Chatterton. So when, in 1912, Chatterton produced his fourth book, *FORE AND AFT, The Story of the Fore and Aft Rig from the Earliest Times to the Present*, he featured Colin Archer and his boats in the chapter on Scandinavia. He extolled the *redningskoite*, both for its original purpose and as a yacht, quoted Archer at length and, most important of all, reproduced the lines of a *redningskoite* over the signature of Colin Archer.

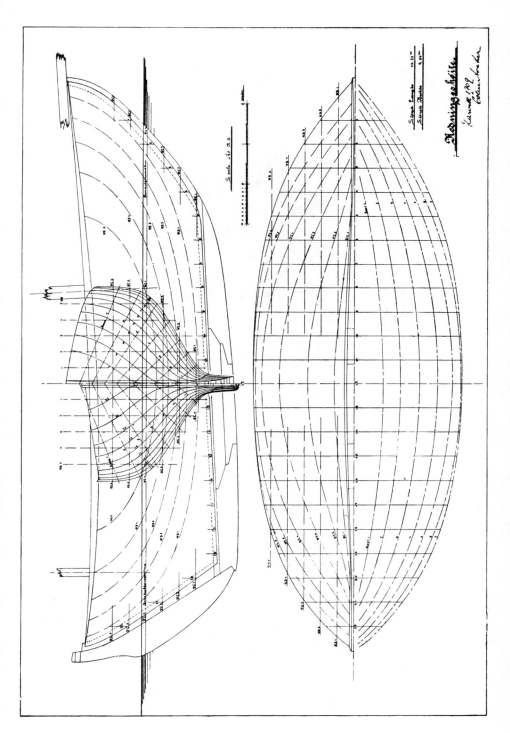

87

LEIV ERIKSSON. A redningskoite *owned by William Washburn Nutting. After crossing the Atlantic in 1924, she was en route from Greenland to Battle Harbour, Labrador, and went missing with the loss of all hands. Nutting and Billy Atkin were instrumental in popularizing the type in the United States.*

Chatterton's book enjoyed a wide circulation in the decade following its publication. On this side of the Atlantic the naval architect William Atkin read it and was sufficiently impressed to design his well-known *Eric,* based on the *redningskoite* lines he saw in the book. What modifications he made to the entry of his *Erics* may well have negated Colin Archer's Wave Form Theory, possibly for the better.

In turn, M. H. Miner designed *Direction* from what he found in Chatterton and laid her keel in 1926. Axel Ingwerson, a Dane employed by the Northern Telegraph Company in Shanghai, built *Shanghai* in 1923. When his job ended in China, he sailed her home to Denmark to become the second recipient of the Cruising Club of America's Blue Water Medal.

After William Washburn Nutting, founder of the Cruising Club of America and one-time editor of *Rudder,* had crossed the Atlantic in the Atkin-designed *Typhoon* in 1920, he became enamored of the *redningskoite* type through the influence of Atkin. In 1924 he purchased a *redningskoite* in Norway and named her *Leiv Eriksson*. He sailed her to Iceland and Greenland, and then he and his crew were lost on the passage to Labrador.

So we find that although the work of Colin Archer was well known in Scandinavia, it took Chatterton to introduce him to English-speaking people, and it took the publicity of *Shanghai's* passage from China to Denmark, plus the design work of William Atkin, to arouse an interest in the type in the United States.

In 1967 the British naval architect W. I. B. Crealock designed a fiberglass mold based on the Atkin *Eric*. This was acquired in 1971 by the Westsail Corporation and has since been used to produce the Westsail 32.

In 1973 the Colin Archer Club of Stockholm, Sweden, built the mold for a 39-foot fiberglass *redningskoite* which is available to its members and the general public for building boats on a do-it-yourself basis.

The COLIN ARCHER 40,
the modern version of the redningskoite.

A fiberglass hull made from molds owned by the Colin Archer Club of Stockholm, Sweden, P.O. Box 496, S-1010-26, Stockholm, Sweden. Membership in the club entitles a person to borrow the mold long enough to build a hull.

William P. (Billy) Atkin

*The following is an excerpt from a letter
sent to Carl Vilas from John Atkin, dated
June 11, 1975: "Here is a photo of Billy
that I took when he was about 72 — we
were on a 'land cruise' Down East. This
was taken at Pemaquid Point."*

WILLIAM ATKIN

WILLIAM ATKIN is perhaps the American designer most responsible for spreading the popularity of the Norwegian *redningskoite*,
or rescue boat, in the United States. Henry D. Bixby, of the Long
Island boatbuilding firm of Chute and Bixby, who built Atkin's
early double-enders, described the first three boats (dubbed *Faith*,
Hope, and *Charity*) in an article he wrote for the March 1927
issue of *Fore An' Aft* magazine. Let me quote: "*Freya* (one of
them) was adapted from a 47-foot Colin Archer *redningskoite* by
Billy Atkin, at the request of the late Bill Nutting. *Freya* differed
in having a shorter keel, less forefoot, and by being fined out
forward on the water line but not on deck. Beyond that, she was
the Archer boat, proportionally reduced to 32 feet overall. The
proportionate reduction cut her draft a bit too much, so she was
given five feet draft. It might be well to add that her beam was
11 feet on deck and 9 feet 10 inches on the water line. *Dragon*
was another of the same dimensions but she retained the deep forefoot and full bow of the original Colin Archer *redningskoite*."

I might add parenthetically that when *Freya* was owned by the late George Richards, former commodore of the Cruising Club of America, she was faster than *Direction,* but that was before I added a ton of inside ballast to *Direction.* Today she might be faster, or at least be able to hold her own with the "Atkinized" Colin Archer design.

Atkin was by no means the first to recognize the merits of the double-ender. Albert Strange, a 19th-century English yacht designer, drew up a set of plans for his fellow Englishman Claud Worth which appeared in Worth's *Yacht Cruising,* first published in 1910 and republished as late as 1934. Strange's double-ender had a much rounder stern at the deck than the Colin Archer stern which is nearly pointed. Albert Strange's fame came with his "canoe stern," which had an inboard rudderpost.

Some years later John G. Hanna designed his world-famous 30-foot Tahiti ketch and his less-well-known 36-foot version, the *Carol.* These, however, should not be confused with the Colin Archer *redningskoite.* Hanna explains in the May 1939 issue of *Rudder:* "I spent most of the hours and dollars of three years in accumulating an immense mass of plans and data about all the world's double-enders . . . sifting out the best ideas from all, and welding them to my own individual personal concept of what would be a good double-ender."

Weston Farmer elaborated still further on the origins of the Tahiti ketch in an article in the *National Fisherman* in which he explained that the boat was first designed under the name *Neptune* for Mr. Anton Schneider of Lakeland, Florida, sometime in 1923. In the early 1930's Farmer was the editor of *Mechanix Illustrated* magazine and ordered a design for a home-built boat from John Hanna, who eventually submitted the plans for *Neptune.* Weston Farmer chose the name *Tahiti* because a member of his staff had been vacationing there. Under the name *Neptune* the same plans appeared in *Rudder,* but Weston Farmer closes his argument with, "If anyone knows the true story of *Tahiti* née *Neptune* and her genesis and midwifery, it should be the midwife who brought her into the world. That fellow was I."

Starting back in 1926 with his three Erics—*Freya, Valgerda* and *Eric*—William S. Atkin populated the oceans with modified Colin Archer types which are probably the only serious rivals to Hanna's Tahiti ketch for most circumnavigations, ocean-crossings and awards of the Cruising Club of America's Blue Water Medal.

FREYA, one of the three "Eric" designs by Billy Atkin built by Chute & Bixby at Huntingdon (Long Island), New York. They were dubbed "Faith, Hope & Charity," by the boatbuilding crew that worked on them, but were named FREYA, VALGERDA and ERIC by their owners. FREYA was flagship of the CCA in 1951 under the ownership of George H. Richards.

Plans of Cutter "DIRECTION"

DESIGNED BY
M. H. MINER
NEW YORK

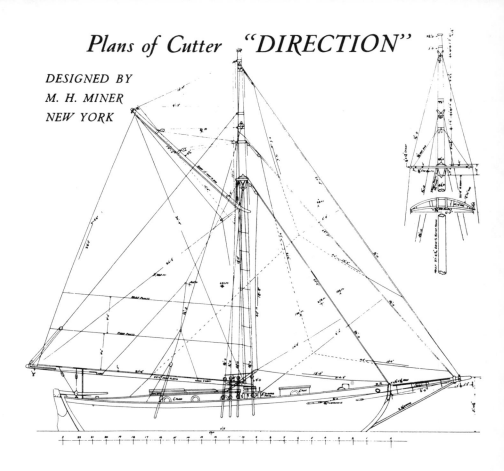

PLANS AND OFFSETS OF *DIRECTION*

IN THE PREFACE, I mentioned that this would be a book for browsing; that our cabin conversations would range over many subjects; and that some might interest one reader and some another.

The lines and plans which follow may be of interest to many readers, but only if you are a naval architect or a shipbuilder will the table of offsets mean anything to you. The table of offsets, however, is the key that will make possible the reproduction of Direction, tomorrow or a century hence. Therefore it is included for the benefit of posterity and to make compete the handiwork of M.H. Miner, whose skill it records but whose dream never came to fruition. With these drawings and a knowledge of lofting and shipbuilding, the redningskoite type could become immortal.

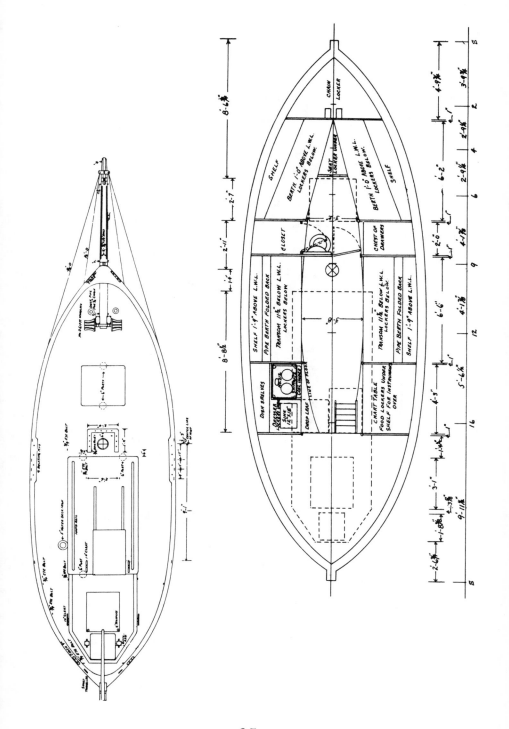

95

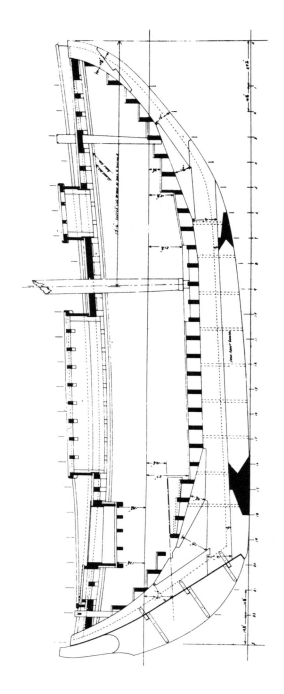

96

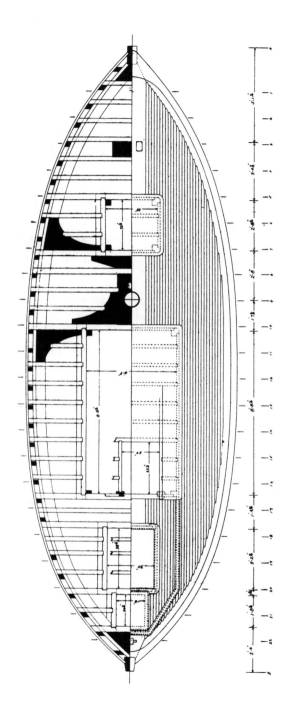

97

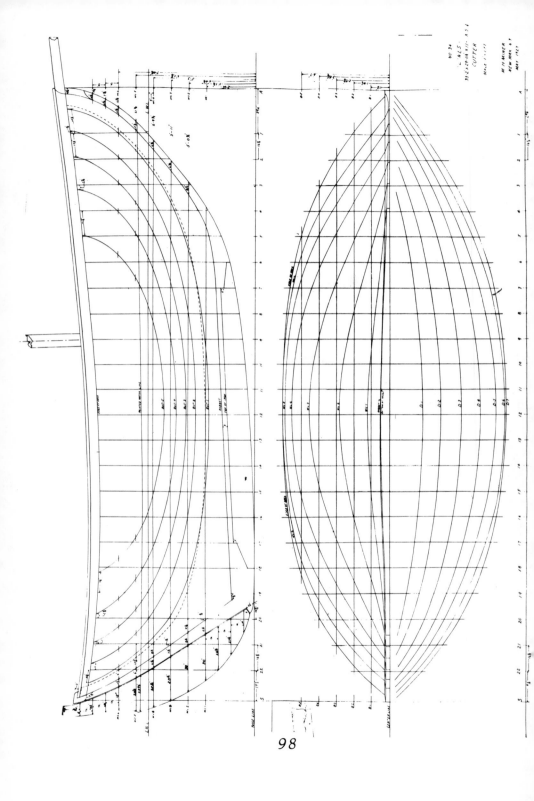

98

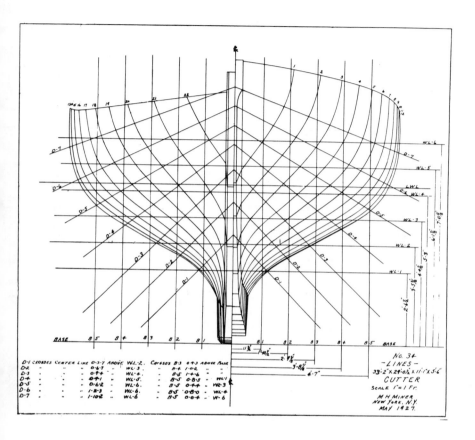

NOTE: The lines and body plans of Direction were originally drawn to a scale of one inch to the foot. To fit these pages they have necessarily been reduced to varying scales. To return to the original scale, enlarge them until the distance from the load water-line to the baseline equals five and a half inches. This may require more than one step in an enlarger but when you are done you will have drawings scaled one inch per foot as they were originally drawn by Mr. Miner. They will then show a draft of 5 feet when Direction floats on her designed load waterline. However, with the diesel engine and ballast added by me, her actual draft is closer to six feet two inches. Compare the early photographs of her trial runs in the Tappan Zee with contemporary ones and note how much longer and sleeker she looks today and how much more like a Tahiti ketch she looked in 1929.

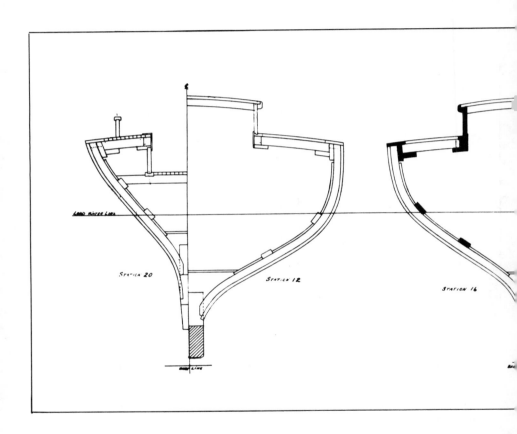

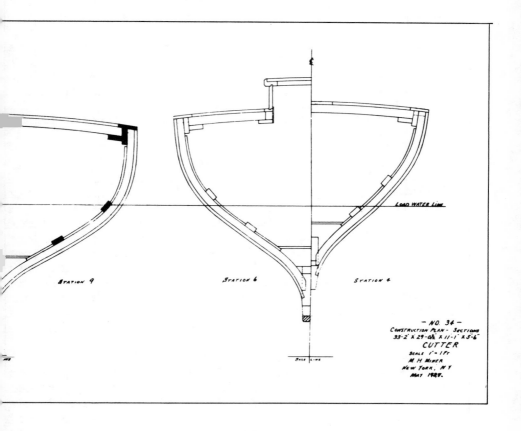

STATION 9

STATION 6

STATION 4

LOAD WATER LINE

BASE LINE

— NO. 34 —
CONSTRUCTION PLAN - SECTIONS
33-2" X 29-0½" X 11-1" X 5-6"
CUTTER
SCALE 1" = 1 FT
M. H. MINER
NEW YORK, N.Y.
MAY 1928.

STATIONS	A	1	2	3	4	5	6	7	8	9

—HEIGHTS—

	A	1	2	3	4	5	6	7	8	9
Sheer To Top Of House Side						1-3-4	1-3-6	1-4-0		
" " " Rail	0-7-0	0-6-6	0-6-5	0-6-4	0-6-3	0-6-2	0-6-1	0-6-0	0-5-7	0-5-6
Base To Sheer	9-10-0	9-6-2	9-4-2	9-2-2	9-0-3	8-10-5	8-8-7	8-7-2	8-5-6	8-4-2
L.W.L. To Painted Water Line		0-7-0	0-6-6	0-6-4	0-6-2	0-6-0	0-5-6	0-5-4	0-5-2	0-5-0
Base To But #5						8-7-7	6-8-2	5-10-3	5-4-3	5-0-3
" " " #4					7-1-3	6-0-7	5-4-4	4-11-0	4-6-6	4-3-7
" " " #3			8-9-4	6-11-2	5-10-4	5-1-7	4-7-5	4-3-1	3-11-5	3-9-2
" " " #2		8-11-3	6-11-3	5-9-5	4-11-7	4-5-0	3-11-7	3-8-1	3-5-1	3-3-1
" " " #1		7-0-6	5-9-4	4-10-1	4-1-7	3-7-7	3-3-1	2-11-5	2-9-1	2-7-1
" " Rabbet		6-0-3	4-10-2	3-9-5	2-11-2	2-4-6	2-1-6	2-0-3	←	- - -
" " Top Of Iron						1-5-5	1-9-2	←		
" " Bottom Of Keel	9-10-0	5-6-7	4-5-0	3-3-7	2-5-1	1-8-7	1-3-5	1-0-3	0-9-6	0-7-6

—HALF BREADTHS—

	A	1	2	3	4	5	6	7	8	9
Sheer		1-11-5	2-10-4	3-7-0	4-2-0	4-7-3	4-11-1	5-2-1	5-4-2	5-5-3
Water Line #6		0-11-5	1-11-3	2-10-3	3-7-5	4-3-0	4-8-4	5-0-3	5-3-1	5-5-0
" " #5		0-4-0	1-3-2	2-2-0	3-0-1	3-8-6	4-3-5	4-8-6	5-0-4	5-2-6
" " #4			0-6-4	1-4-3	2-1-6	2-10-4	3-6-3	4-0-5	4-5-6	4-9-2
" " #3				0-6-6	1-2-0	1-9-3	2-4-3	2-10-7	3-4-2	3-8-3
" " #2					0-5-3	0-9-3	1-1-7	1-6-3	1-10-7	2-2-3
" " #1						0-3-7	0-5-4	0-7-3	0-9-2	0-11-0
Rabbet	0-3-0	0-3-0	0-3-0	0-3-0	0-3-0	0-3-3	0-3-6	0-4-1	0-4-6	0-5-1
Bottom Of Keel	0-3-0	0-0-7	0-1-2	0-1-4	0-2-0	0-2-3	0-3-0	0-3-6	0-4-3	0-4-7

—DIAGONALS—

	A	1	2	3	4	5	6	7	8	9
Diagonal #7		1-4-3	2-8-0	2-5-3	4-1-2	4-7-5	5-0-6	5-4-5	5-7-4	5-9-4
" #6		1-5-4	2-3-6	3-0-6	3-8-7	4-3-6	4-9-2	5-2-0	5-5-4	5-7-7
" #5		1-1-1	1-10-6	2-7-3	3-3-0	3-9-5	4-3-1	4-7-4	4-11-1	5-2-0
" #4		0-8-5	1-5-5	2-1-6	2-8-6	3-2-3	3-7-2	3-11-2	4-2-3	4-4-7
" #3			0-11-1	1-6-4	2-0-4	2-5-4	2-9-5	3-1-0	3-3-6	3-5-5
" #2				0-9-6	1-2-7	1-7-0	1-10-4	2-1-3	2-3-5	2-5-3
" #1					0-6-7	0-10-1	1-0-7	1-3-1	1-4-7	1-6-2

All Dimensions In Feet, Inches And Eighths To Outside Of Planking.

Base Line 5'-6" Below Load Water Line.

10	11	12	13	14	15	16	17	18	19	20	21	22	S

—HEIGHTS—

10	11	12	13	14	15	16	17	18	19	20	21	22	S
1-4-2	1-4-6	1-5-0	1-5-0	1-4-7	1-4-5	1-4-0	1-2-4	1-0-3	0-10-5	0-8-6	0-7-0		
0-5-5	0-5-4	0-5-3	0-5-2	0-5-1	0-5-0	0-4-7	0-4-6	0-4-5	0-4-4	0-4-3	0-4-2	0-4-1	0-4-0
8-3-1	8-2-1	8-1-3	8-0-6	8-0-3	8-0-0	8-0-0	8-0-3	8-0-6	8-1-5	8-2-7	8-4-3	8-6-2	8-9-0
0-4-6	0-4-4	0-4-2	0-4-0	0-3-6	0-3-4	0-3-4	0-3-6	0-4-0	0-4-2	0-4-4	0-4-6	0-5-0	0-5-2
4-9-7	4-8-3	4-8-0	4-8-7	4-11-0	5-2-2	5-7-2	6-3-6	7-7-2					
4-1-7	4-0-6	4-0-4	4-0-7	4-2-3	4-4-7	4-8-4	5-1-5	5-9-3	6-8-7				
3-7-4	3-6-4	3-6-3	3-6-6	3-7-7	3-9-7	4-0-5	4-4-7	4-10-3	5-6-5	6-6-7			
3-1-5	3-0-6	3-0-4	3-0-7	3-1-6	3-3-1	3-5-3	3-8-5	4-1-3	4-8-0	5-5-7	6-8-6		
2-5-5	2-4-6	2-4-3	2-4-4	2-5-2	2-6-5	2-8-4	2-11-2	3-3-2	3-8-7	4-5-0	5-6-7	7-3-2	
— STRAIGHT TO —			—	—	—	—	→	1-2-2	2-5-4	4-3-3	6-3-0		
— STRAIGHT TO —			—	—	→	1-0-7	0-4-0						
0-6-0	0-4-4	0-3-3	0-2-3	0-1-5	0-1-0	0-0-4	0-0-0	0-0-0	0-0-2	1-3-7	3-4-3	5-5-1	8-9-0

—HALF BREADTHS—

10	11	12	13	14	15	16	17	18	19	20	21	22	S
5-6-1	5-6-4	5-6-4	5-6-2	5-5-5	5-4-4	5-2-5	5-0-0	4-8-0	4-2-5	3-7-1	2-8-5	1-7-3	
5-6-0	5-6-4	5-6-4	5-6-2	5-5-2	5-3-6	5-1-4	4-10-0	4-5-1	3-10-1	3-0-7	2-1-1	0-10-0	
5-4-2	5-5-0	5-5-1	5-4-6	5-3-6	5-1-5	4-10-5	4-5-7	3-11-4	3-3-2	2-5-2	1-5-0		
4-11-2	5-0-5	5-0-7	5-0-2	4-10-4	4-7-4	4-3-1	3-9-3	3-2-3	2-5-6	1-7-7	0-9-1		
3-11-5	4-1-4	4-2-0	4-1-0	3-10-6	3-7-0	3-2-1	2-8-3	2-1-6	1-6-5	0-11-1	0-3-5		
2-5-2	2-7-0	2-7-3	2-6-4	2-4-6	2-1-7	1-10-4	1-6-2	1-1-5	0-9-0	0-5-0			
1-0-4	1-1-4	1-1-7	1-1-4	1-0-6	0-11-5	0-10-1	0-8-2	0-6-3	0-4-6	0-3-3			
0-5-4	0-5-7	0-6-1	0-6-1	0-5-7	0-5-5	0-5-0	0-4-4	0-3-7	0-3-3	0-3-3	0-3-3	0-3-3	0-3-3
0-5-3	0-5-5	0-5-5	0-5-5	0-5-3	0-4-7	0-4-4	0-3-7	0-3-1	0-2-7	2-2-5	0-2-5	0-2-5	0-2-5

—DIAGONALS—

10	11	12	13	14	15	16	17	18	19	20	21	22	S
5-10-5	5-11-2	5-11-3	5-11-0	5-9-7	5-8-1	5-5-6	5-2-2	4-9-5	4-3-3	3-7-2	2-8-7	1-7-5	
5-9-4	5-10-3	5-10-5	5-10-2	5-9-1	5-6-7	5-3-6	4-11-3	4-5-7	3-11-2	3-3-1	2-5-1	1-4-0	
5-3-7	5-5-1	5-5-2	5-4-5	5-3-0	5-0-6	4-9-3	4-5-2	4-0-1	3-5-5	2-9-6	2-0-2	0-11-7	
4-6-5	4-7-4	4-7-7	4-7-3	4-6-1	4-4-0	4-1-2	3-9-4	3-5-1	2-11-3	2-4-3	1-7-1	0-7-3	
3-7-2	3-8-0	3-8-1	3-7-6	3-6-7	3-5-3	3-3-1	3-0-1	2-8-2	2-3-4	1-9-3	1-1-2		
2-6-5	2-7-3	2-7-5	2-7-1	2-6-4	2-5-2	2-3-5	2-1-3	1-10-2	1-6-1	1-1-3	0-6-5		
1-7-3	1-8-0	1-8-2	1-8-0	1-7-4	1-6-4	1-5-2	1-3-3	1-1-1	0-10-2	0-7-0			

— NO. 34 —
OFFSET TABLE
33'-2" X 29'-0½" X 11'-1" X 5'-6"
CUTTER
SCALE 1" = 1 FT.
M. H. MINER
NEW YORK
MAY, 1927.

Rockwell Kent

M. H. MINER

M. H. MINER of 2922 Grand Concourse, Bronx, New York City, was a daily commuter by noisy, crowded subway to his office at the New York Telephone Company in hectic Manhattan. He was, most would agree, a man badly in need of a dream. One day in 1926 he consulted William Atkin about designing a boat for a proposed cruise to the South Sea Islands—where there are no subway trains. This tidbit of information was revealed to me by Billy Atkin when I called on him at his combination workshop-home one day in the early 1950's.

However, Mr. Miner eventually decided to design his own boat, and drew up a 33-foot *redningskoite* directly from the Colin Archer lines that were printed in Chatterton's book, *Fore And Aft*. This was the design that became *Direction*. That Miner was a skilled draftsman is attested to by the excellent plans for *Direction* that appear here. It is indeed tragic that Miner's vision of a South Sea Islands paradise was shattered, only to be replaced by the Kent-Allen dream.

Kent's version of the tragedy he conceded to be fictional, but he may well have come closer to the truth than he knew. Let me quote from the last lines on page seven of *N by E:*

". . . so at almost the very moment that this poor man was to step into his swan boat, his wife, we only guess, confronted him.

'What,'—arms akimbo—'do you think you're going to do in that boat?'

'I was going,' he answered with quiet determination, 'to sail to Par—to the South Seas.'

'You're not.'

And there, true or not, ends one of the saddest stories in the world."

104

DIRECTION at her launching, Nyack, New York, 1929.

SIDNEY MILLER

I CALLED ON Sidney Miller at his home in Nyack, New York in the 1950's. It was he who actually built *Direction*. I went there hoping to learn more about Mr. Miner, but Sidney Miller was in an advanced stage of palsy, quite hard of hearing, and able to utter only a few intelligible words at a time. His mind was keen, however, and everything that he could hear registered; he responded with smiles and barely audible comments which his wife interpreted for me.

I showed him photographs of *Direction* from my wallet and he studied them with interest. I could just barely understand the words "fifty" and "mast" which Mrs. Miller interpreted as "I put a fifty cent piece under her mast when we stepped it." One outcome of this visit was to have Mrs. Miller and her son, John, and his family from Renton, Washington, go for a sail on *Direction* when John came East on his vacation. Another result was my receiving a dandy picture of *Direction* taken right before her launching. For me it was a most rewarding contact, and I like to think that poor, ailing Sidney Miller got some pleasure out of it, too.

105

The late Arthur S. Allen, Sr.
Photograph courtesy of his niece,
Mrs. Georgia North Newcomb.

ARTHUR S. ALLEN SR.

AS I'VE NOTED, during the winter of 1918-19, when I was 11 years old, my family lived at Philipse Manor, New York. The Allens were our neighbors; young Art and I commuted by train up the Hudson River to the Scarborough School, while our fathers commuted downriver to their jobs in New York City. Art and I were constant playmates that winter and the following spring. When we were older we used to meet when our schools were football rivals.

Ten years later, Art Allen was sailing his yawl, *Anaqua*, to Baddeck, while I was making a less ambitious cruise in my cat-boat, *Nancy Lee*, through the old Delaware and Raritan Canal, down Chesapeake Bay to Washington, D.C. Neither of us knew of the other's interest in boats, but, by coincidence, my first cruising article appeared in the July 1929 issue of *Yachting*, the same one that carried Lucius Beebe's press release about *Direction's* proposed cruise.

Reading the correspondence between my chum, Art, then studying naval architecture at M.I.T., and his father, I marvel at the energy and ambition displayed by them in purchasing *Direction* when she was still incomplete and getting her to sea in just four months. A thousand and one jobs lay between those two events, and most of them had to be discussed and directed by letter. It is small wonder that *Direction* was overrigged and underballasted. Something had to be wrong!

Art's father was a dynamic personality and successful in business, but he was not a sailor. He had to rely on the advice of others when it came to helping his son prepare *Direction* for sea. How natural for him to expect that Albert Thorsen, a retired rigger of clipper ships, should be qualified to rig *Direction*. But Thorsen had never before rigged a small yacht, hence the ⅝-inch wire standing rigging and spars weighing close to a ton. By the time Art Allen came to realize these mistakes he and his crew were already crossing Cabot Strait and past the point of no return.

There were personality conflicts aboard *Direction* not only on the trip but before *Direction* ever left Nyack, N. Y. But Art's father never forgave Kent for disclosing this with his disparaging remarks about "Cupid" in *N by E*. As a result Mr. Allen's friends (who were also Kent's friends) published a privately printed book to relate Art's version of the cruise. They were Tom Cleland, Rudolph Ruzicka and Sydney Bagshaw, all names to be reckoned with in the field of graphic arts. *Under Sail To Greenland* was printed by the Marchbanks Press with three hundred copies for private use and six hundred for sale by the printer.

The book still appears in the catalogs of the antiquarian book dealers. It makes good reading, especially if you have *N by E* alongside and compare both versions. For example:

From *N by E* "More speed!" says the skipper. Up goes the spinnaker. "For God's sake, don't put that on," I protest.

From *Under Sail to Greenland* "I shook out the reefs and set the spinnaker (qualms from Rockwell) and we went along very fast."

Rockwell Kent aboard the square-rigged ship LONSDALE at Punta Arenas, Patagonia, in the Straits of Magellan, 1922. He was 40 years old at the time and was converting one of the ship's open lifeboats to the decked-over cruising sloop KATHLEEN shown on the opposite page. In her he made an unsuccessful attempt to reach Cape Horn. Out of this adventure came his second illustrated travel book, VOYAGING SOUTH FROM THE STRAITS OF MAGELLAN, a revised edition of which was published by Grosset and Dunlap as recently as 1968.

KATHLEEN

ROCKWELL KENT

Yachts other than *Direction* have made the voyage to Greenland and have returned without incident. Wright Britton and his navigator wife, Patricia, sailed to Godthaab in 1965 in their yawl *Delight*. Others who have been there more recently were H. W. Tilman, George Moffett, Thomas J. Watson Jr. and E. Newbold Smith. Nothing, however, has been published about these voyages to stir the imagination of the general public as did the account of the naively conducted cruise of *Direction* as related in *N by E*. Why? The answer is Rockwell Kent.

Rockwell Kent could communicate. Communication is more than a mere transfer of information. Communication on the level of great artists of any medium is the communication of feeling, the ability to quicken your pulse and awaken a zest for living. Such is the communication of a Kipling, a Beethoven, or a Michaleangelo, to name but a few. Yes, and even Rockwell Kent.

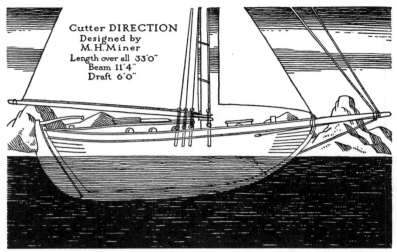

Cutter DIRECTION
Designed by
M. H. Miner
Length over all 33'0"
Beam 11'4"
Draft 6'0"

Rockwell Kent

My wife and I had the good fortune some years ago to spend a weekend in Au Sable Forks, New York, at "Asgaard," the home of Rockwell Kent and his wife, Sally. When we entered the living room, there over the mantel was a scene of Greenland with a Greenlandic girl in the foreground surrounded by mountains and a cerulean sky. It was a great work of art: No one had to tell me so, nor did I need an art education to recognize that fact.

It struck me with a palpable force; it was the stuff of genius, the work of a master. The master's politics and mine probably were a mile apart. I dare say that our moral codes were equally polarized, but through that picture he penetrated to the innermost me.

In creating *N. by E.* Rockwell Kent's medium might be said to have been the *complete* book. It encompassed art not only in the sense that he produced striking woodcuts that were reproducible on the printed page, but, of equal importance, is his prose and the philosophy it expressed. Cover design and layout welded the whole into one harmonious, integrated unit. However, there had to be more than a book to produce the impact of a best seller. It takes two to communicate: Kent found a receptive audience in a civilized society still not that far removed—as the eons are counted—from its cave-man ancestors. That spirit of adventure, freedom, glamor and romance, which had survival quality in the not-too-dim past, is easily re-awakened in us by a man with Kent's gift for communication.

110

Rockwell Kent

Rockwell Kent

Three woodcuts Rockwell Kent created for his book N by E, his story of DIRECTION'S cruise to Greenland. Courtesy the Rockwell Kent Legacies.

In the 1920's, the deepest longings and desires of most of us were suppressed almost to the bursting point by the remnants of a Victorian culture, but in Rockwell Kent we find an individual with no such burden of inhibitions. Fifty years before it became fashionable he was openly practicing free love, and was roaming to the very ends of the earth. Fifty years before the word "establishment" took on its present connotations he was against it. Many others have done the same, but they did not have his gift for communication. It has been charged that Rockwell Kent was a selfish man, inconsiderate and self-centered. This might be translated as saying that to excel in the areas in which he did, one must have a singleness of purpose that permits absolutely nothing to stand in its way. If the end result is that, through his creativity, you and I gain a safety valve for the release of our pent-up primordial urges, and thereby are able to find meaning and purpose in otherwise dull and humdrum lives, then I say we were fortunate, indeed, to have Rockwell Kent pass our way.

Mrs. George (Sunny) Greenberg of Sarasota, Florida,
took this happy photograph of Rockwell Kent in
late 1970 when he had but a few months to live.

113

PART III:
Memorabilia

FROM THE *DIRECTION* SCRAPBOOK

During the 30 years since I purchased *Direction,* a mass of material has flowed to me from many places and many people, as if I were a magnet to the iron filings of far-flung stories of the boat, its cruise to Greenland, and the people involved with her. Gradually I've organized the material and put it into scrapbooks. It gives me considerable pleasure to browse through this collection occasionally, and to relive, vicariously, a story which began over four decades ago with my boyhood chum as the central character in the drama.

Sifting through this material, something else emerges that I find fascinating: It recalls sharply the way the world was in my youth, an age before transatlantic air service, before television, when the telephone was still fairly new, when ships took a week or more to cross the Atlantic. I see how all these facts of daily life affected the unfolding drama of *Direction,* once she was wrecked in that Greenland fjord.

How casually we accept today's vast and sophisticated methods of instant communication with any part of the world, yet how slow and frustrating such communication was only as far back as 1929, when the families of *Direction's* crew were anxiously seeking word of the safety of those aboard the shipwrecked boat.

The younger we are the more intensely we live for the present and the less we are concerned with the past. Until I was approaching the age of 60, I never more than glanced at my accumulating documents concerning *Direction.* I was just too busy. This is where the historian fits in. He has the time and interest to sift, sort and select from dusty records just the barest material necessary to share with you the thrill of his own full time occupation of delving into history. Possibly if you are under 50, you could not care less about the past. If so, you may skip to the next section where action resumes that could be applied to your own boat. I would be remiss, however, not to share with older readers some of the documents that give a first hand glimpse of life as it was in the early days of *Direction.* Let me lay out on the cabin table, just a few pages of my voluminous scrapbook.

To begin with I have a letter dated June 17, 1951, addressed to "The owner of the yawl [sic] *Direction*, Essex, Conn." This reached me because an imaginative postal clerk passed it on to the Essex Paint and Marine company of Essex, Connecticut, where E. Van Dyke Wetmore, its proprietor, held it for my next visit. It reads:

> Dear Mr. Vilas,
>
> Ever since I read an account of your acquiring *Direction* in *Yachting*, I have been intending to write and offer you some maps and the log of Arthur Allen's trip to Greenland. I happen to have these, and hate to discard them if they would be of interest to you as the present owner of the boat.
>
> (Signed) Harry J. Calnan
152 East 94th St.
New York 28, N.Y.

Mr. Calnan's wife was Arthur S. Allen's secretary at the time of his death in 1945 and the article he refers to was the one titled "*Direction* Heads Home" appearing in the first part of this book. I responded with a phone call and a visit to the Calnan apartment, returning home with the nucleus of my future collection.

In its present scrapbook form it begins with a notation of how Allen senior was weekending with Kent and the artist Tom Cleland at *Asgaard*, the Kent home in the Adirondacks. As they sat around the fire in the evening Kent asked where Allen's son was going next summer. Allen said he was not sure, but thought probably to Cape Breton or Newfoundland.

"May I go with him," Kent asked.

So Allen wrote his son who was attending the School of Naval Architecture at M.I.T., and got the following reply, "Opportunities of real worth do not knock at the door every day, nor every year, and life is too short to pass them up without consideration. I should like to cruise with Rockwell Kent next summer more than anything else."

Rockwell Kent wrote to "Sam"—as Art was called in later years— on November 19, 1928: ". . . Now that you will take me on your trip you may consider my acceptance as dependable as the Rock of Gibralter. Don't look upon me as a sailor in any expert sense. . . . A few years ago I was one of a crowd that was to sail from

SHANGHAI. A Colin Archer redningskoite *that did much to popularize the type around the world when she sailed from Shanghai to Denmark, for which her owner, Axel Ingwersen, was awarded the second Blue Water Medal by the Cruising Club of America. From a painting by Clayton Slawter.*

Denmark to America by way of Iceland and Greenland. For aggravated personal reasons, and because of my conviction that the trip was being mismanaged, I left the enterprise at Copenhagen. My hunch was sound, for they lost the boat and almost their own lives on the coast of Nova Scotia through what seemed to be stupid navigation. . . ."

The yacht referred to in Kent's letter was the ketch *Shanghai,* purchased in 1924 by Judge F. De Witt Wells. Her passage from Denmark to Greenland and her wreck in Nova Scotia is described in Wells' book *The Last Cruise of the Shanghai.* Among the iron filings that my magnet has collected on these events is a batch of Xerox copies of the correspondence concerning that cruise in the handwriting of Wells and other principals. Digress with me just a moment for a glimpse of the other side of the coin — in the words of Chanler Chapman, nephew of Wells and a crew member on that memorable voyage. This excerpt is from an 11-page letter:

119

On Board *Shanghai*
June 26, 1924.

. . . let me say a word or two about Rockwell Kent. Both
Bette Evans and Wigham (the editor of *Town And
Country*) shook their heads doubtfully when I said that
he was coming. He has a big reputation as an after-dinner
raconteur and as big a reputation for exaggerating and
for playing his friends for suckers. Judge Wells met him
in New York right after his exhibition of pictures, which
had not too much of a financial success.

Kent's wife and children are at Antibes, France. The
Judge told him that he proposed buying a small ocean-
going sailboat and sailing to Sardinia. Out of the goodness
of his heart he proposed to take two second-class tickets
on the *Homeric* instead of one first class for himself alone,
and invited Kent along . . .

Kent then went on to Antibes to visit his family while
Judge Wells purchased the *Shanghai* in Copenhagen . . . .
Kent arrived at Copenhagen the day before I did—
June 23rd. The first night we all went to supper in the
Tivoli . . . . We were five, the two others being two of
the three Danes who had sailed *Shanghai* from China.
Kent explained that he had been spending five days
with a friend in Germany, and that Germany was the
greatest country in the world. . . . This did not please
the Danes and of course it rubbed the Judge and myself
the wrong way. . . . About an hour after dinner Kent
drew me aside and said that he did not think he could
get on with the Judge and that he did not want to make
the trip. . . . Such is a brief sketch of why Kent did not
come and, oh, God, aren't we glad he didn't!

It is worth noting that—without further word to his host, who
had paid his fare across the Atlantic—Kent slipped away at that
very moment and disappeared, on the eve of their departure.

Returning to my own files, here's a letter by M.H. Miner, who
designed *Direction* and sold her to the Allens, written to Allen Sr.
on December 2, 1928: ". . . I claim no credit for the lines of this
ship as they are an *exact* copy of Colin Archer's famous *redningskoite* design."

120

Rockwell Kent wrote to Sam on February 12, 1929: "I'll be more than happy to carve the name of the boat for bow and stern—carve it and illuminate it. We'll make that part worthy of the rest." He did so, and when we moved aboard *Direction* in July 1946, Walter Pinaud salvaged one of those Kent-carved name-boards from the rubbish heap in his boatyard. I reconditioned it and later presented it to Mystic Seaport, where for many years it was on display in the main dining room of the Seaport Inne.

Next in my scrapbook are several pages of newspaper clippings dated May 18, 1929, from the *New York Sun*, the *Tarrytown Daily News* and the *New York Times*. "LOCAL BOYS SAIL TOMORROW WITH ROCKWELL KENT, THREE FRIENDS ON TRIP TO GREENLAND" read the headlines, with drop heads of "Arthur Allen to be gone for six months"; "Boat Built at Nyack Especially for Trip"; "Only Sails To Be Used."

The story includes pictures of *Direction*, Arthur Allen Jr., Lucian Cary Jr. and Edward Crofutt, the third crewman for the trip to Baddeck. Some of these clippings are from what the Calnans gave me, others from a collection I've kept since 1929.

Direction departed for Baddeck, Nova Scotia, but her skipper was still finishing his final year at M.I.T. On May 20, 1929, he wrote to his father: ". . . what is the idea of sending publicity? We will get plenty of that when we get back." Then, after hearing that *Direction* had an encounter with a barge going through Hell Gate, another letter, written May 23, 1929, to his father starts off: "It's rotten hard on you to get tardy phone calls from June that he hit something. I'm worried, too, and surely hope the hull is not strained."

How *Direction* ever navigated the East River and Hell Gate without an engine is beyond me. Alf Loomis also would agree: as he tells in his article, he hired a tugboat to tow *Direction* through Hell Gate in 1931, so perhaps Cary should get credit for some pretty good boat-handling.

When Admiral Peary (with MacMillan and Bartlett) returned from the North Pole in 1909 in the *Roosevelt*, their first port of call was Battle Harbour, Labrador, because it was the farthest north wireless telegraph station and communication with the outside world. That is why *Shanghai* under Judge Wells, and *Liev Eriksson* under Bill Nutting, both headed for the same port on their way from Greenland in 1924. It was still the same in 1929 when Arthur Allen Sr. made inquiries of the Western Union Telegraph Company as to the best mode of communication. The Western Union reply was a series of letters and a map with a red line sketched in, showing a telegraph wire running from Quebec to Chateau Bay, Labrador, and a cable across to Belle Isle. Battle Harbour, on another island, had wireless contact with St. Johns, Newfoundland, and operated the year around. But the only communication with Greenland was by cable from New York to England, thence by cable to Iceland and, finally, by wireless on to Greenland, which had wireless offices at Julianehaab, Ivigtut, Godthaab and Godhavn.

My scrapbook now changes from letters and newspaper clippings to telegrams:

Postal Telegraph (The Mackay System):
"BATTLEHARBORNFL (Battle Harbour Newfoundland) via FOGONF (Fogo, Newfoundland) JULY 3, 1929. MR. ARTHUR ALLEN, 230 PARK AVE., NEW YORK: SAIL GREENLAND TOMORROW ALL WELL LETTER FOLLOWS LOVE TO MOTHER.   SAM 6:35 PM"

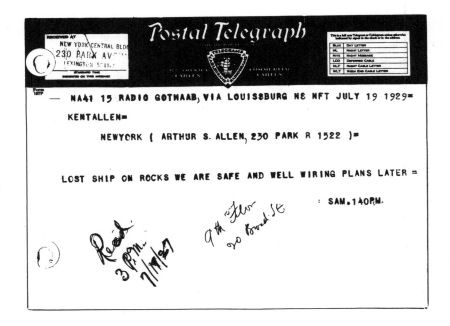

Rockwell Kent

SHIPWRECK

The next telegram:

Postal Telegraph (The Mackay System):
"RADIO GODTHAAB VIA LOUISBURG NS. NFT JULY 19, 1929. KENTALLEN NEW YORK ARTHUR S. ALLEN 230 PARK AVE NEW YORK. LOST SHIP ON ROCKS STOP WE ARE SAFE AND WELL STOP WIRING PLANS LATER.   SAM 1:40 PM"

Then to Frances Kent addressed as above:
"WRECKED ALAMY LOGEN COPENHAGEN ETAPE LOVUS IDO. 1:38 PM."

Since this was in code there is a translation as follows:

WRECKED..Wrecked
ALAMY..........................Everything and everybody all well
LOGEN ....Shall remain there until
COPENHAGEN ....Copenhagen
ETAPE...Can you meet me?
LOVUS...............Do not start until you hear from me again
IDO.......................I do love you (the private code between
              the Kents)

123

The next cable is a copy of one sent to Copenhagen by Arthur Allen, using his code name and address. It reads:

"US MINISTER COPENHAGEN DENMARK JULY 21, 1929. SMALL AMERICAN BOAT WRECKED AT GODTHAAB GREENLAND STOP KENT ALLEN CARY SAVED STOP CAN YOU HELP THEM AND NOTIFY ME?   KENTALLEN"

Then came two pages of clippings from various New York newspapers, carrying such headlines as: "ALLEN YACHT IS LOST ON GREENLAND ROCKS." "ALLEN YACHT PILES UP OFF GREENLAND." The drop heads read: "Laconic Message Tells of Its Loss on Rocks." "22-Year Old Skipper and Crew of Two Safe." There were pictures of Kent, Cary and *Direction*, the same ones that had appeared in May. Since the cables supplied only the barest information, the text of the newspaper articles consisted of speculation and recaps of the previous press releases.

But Arthur Allen was not through. His next telegram reads:

"STATE DEPT. WASH. DC. JULY 21, 1929. BOAT DI-RECTION FROM NEW YORK WAS WRECKED AT GODTHAAB GREENLAND WITH ROCKWELL KENT AND TWO COMPANIONS ABOARD JULY 19 STOP THEY WERE SAVED BUT WE HAVE NO FURTHER WORD STOP CAN YOU HELP US GET WORD FROM OR TO THEM AND WHAT IS THE BEST WAY TO GET THEM BACK?
                    ARTHUR S. ALLEN, 230 Park Ave."

Next, Allen Sr. sent a cable on July 22 to Greenland as follows:

"KENTALLEN GODTHAAB DELAY IPAHO FRADO ISBOZ JELAG. DAD"

This telegraph code translates as follows:

DELAY ....Delay
IPAHO ....Is causing a great deal of anxiety.
FRADO............Are you in need of any assistance that I can render?
ISBOZ........Keep me well informed as to your movements.
JELAG................Please give this your immediate attention.
DAD ....Dad.

124

ALLEN YACHT IS LOST ON GREENLAND ROCKS

22-Year-Old Skipper and Crew of Two, Rockwell Kent, Artist, and Lucian Cary Jr., Are Safe.

A VOYAGE OF ADVENTURE

Three, All Expert Sailors, Started in 33-Foot Direction on Cruise of Discovery.

By The Associated Press.

COPENHAGEN, July 19. — The American yacht Direction, in which Rockwell Kent and two young companions have been exploring the North, was wrecked last Sunday near Godthaab, Greenland, according to a telegram today from that settlement. The crew of three were safe, but the yacht was a total loss.

Crew Sturdy Adventurers.

Word of the loss of the Direction, presumably on the rocks outside the harbor of Godthaab, Greenland, was received here yesterday afternoon by Arthur S. Allen, color engineer, the father of the youthful skipper of the ship, Arthur S. Allen Jr. of Phillipse Manor, Tarrytown, N. Y. A cablegram from his 22-year-old son, laconically announcing: "Lost ship on rocks—we are safe and well," and a garbled message from Mr. Kent, confirming the former message, was all that Mr. Allen knew of the disaster. Both messages were sent from Godthaab.

Mr. Allen expressed the utmost confidence in the ability of his son to handle his ship in all sorts of weather, regardless of tides and wind, and felt sure that some element, such as a thick fog, was accountable for the vessel going on the rocks. In all his years of sailing, which have been many for one of his age, young Allen had never had a disaster, according to his father.

In a letter received by Mr. Allen from the young voyager only a few days ago, written from Battle Harbor, Labrador, on July 3, the young man spoke of hard weather encountered throughout the trip, with two northeast gales and heavy ice and fog.

The letter read, in part:

"The ice is only just out of the harbors and much ice is reported further down the Labrador coast. We have seen many large and impressive bergs.

"My plans are as follows: To go out to sea tomorrow, all set and supplied and tuned up and lashed down. I am going to Godthaab, Greenland, from here as fast as I possibly can. I allow ten days for this passage of about 850 miles. From there I hope to work north along the coast as far as time permits. We will rest there at Godthaab—Rockwell wants to paint.

YACHT DIRECTION, WRECKED NEAR GREENLAND.

Photo by Norman A. Burke.

The stanch ship was manned by Rockwell Kent, artist; Arthur S. Allen Jr. and Lucian Cary Jr. It left Nyack, N. Y., on May 19 for a three-month cruise to Greenland.

Bachrach Photo.
LUCIAN CARY JR.,
Also of the Direction's Crew.

Times Wide World Photos.
ROCKWELL KENT,
Artist, One of the Direction's Crew.

"It is remarkable and delightful how well this cruise is going, how smoothly we work together, how ably our ship stands up. I am learning knowledge of a nature that can be had through no other form of venture or experience.

Ran Into Terrific Storms.

"We are healthy, happy, satisfied. The ship has done what I asked at all times. Nothing whatever has been carried away, not one rope yarn. We have encountered hard weather since Braddeck, and have made exhaustive tests on the ship in

Continued on Page Four.

The response from young Sam to his father reads:
"GODTHAAB VIA BELLEISLNFLD (BELLE ISLE, NEWFOUNDLAND) JULY 22 KENTALLEN NEW YORK SEND DIRECTION PLANS GREENLAND DIRECTOR COPENHAGEN IMMEDIATELY STOP HOME DENMARK STEAMER SEPTEMBER STOP
                                                            SAM."

Arthur Allen Sr. then received this wire, collect from Washington, D.C.:
"ARTHUR S. ALLEN 230 PARK AVE NY RE YOUR TELEGRAM JULY 21 STOP AMERICAN LEGATION COPENHAGEN INSTRUCTED TO ENDEAVOR TO COMMUNICATE WITH KENT AND TO CABLE INFORMATION STOP HENRY L. STIMSON SECY OF STATE."

There are many more cables, too numerous to print, until we come to this one from Rockwell Kent to Arthur Allen Sr.:

"SAM ....SAM
EFDOT...Has started for home
AFAJO ....Expect to arrive at
COPEN...Copenhagen
CICGO ....Last week in August
ALAMY...........................Everything and everybody well
DIRECTION...*Direction*
ALCRE.................................Has had a serious accident
ALCOC ....Have had a consultation of physicians
ALBLY.............................Expect she will be out again by
JUNE...June
ROCKWELL .... Rockwell"

Next is a letter from Herbert L. Stone, editor of *Yachting*, to Arthur Allen Sr. which closes: "Tell your son to be sure to come and see me when he returns. I would like to talk over the trip with him and also the story."

By coincidence I, too, was in contact with Herbert Stone at that time. Sometime during the winter of 1928-29 I had visited *Yachting* with my very first magazine article, and had received a friendly and inspiring reception from Herbert L. Stone. He sat me down in his office, complimented me on my writing and box camera photography, and, as I mentioned before, ran my story of *Nancy Lee* in the same issue with Lucius Beebe's press release about *Direction*. I was pleased to receive the lead position in the magazine, and assumed that Sam had seen my article, as I had seen the one about his boat. But years later his father told me that he had clipped out the Beebe press release and mailed it to Sam without the rest of the magazine. I had looked forward to a reunion with Sam, but alas, that was never to be.

Following is a cheerful cable:

"KOBENHAVEN AUG 20 1929 KENTALLEN NY STOP COPENHAGEN DELIGHTFUL STOP SAIL HOME SEVEN DAYS NEED MONEY STOP ROCKWELL HAS FIVE HUNDRED STOP DENMARK REPAIRING DIRECTION STOP SEND PLANS GREENLAND DIRECTOR IMMEDIATELY STOP I AM ORDERING TIMBERS HERE WILL CABLE PASSAGE DATE AND AMOUNT NEEDED TOMORROW PASSAGE FROM IVIGTUT FINE FOOD GOOD HEALTH PERFECT.
SAM"

The next day Sam sent still another cable to his father:

"SAIL FREDERICK EIGHT THURSDAY AUGUST TWENTYNINE STOP SEND TWO HUNDRED DOLLARS AT ONCE CARE AMERICAN CONSUL ALL FINE.   SAM."

In pencil there is a notation in Mr. Allen's handwriting: "Scandinavian American Line 6th St., Hoboken, N.J. Sails from Copenhagen Aug. 20. Arrives Sept. 9. Takes 11 days."

The senior Allen replied to his son:

"CABLES RECEIVED STOP SENDING TWO HUNDRED TONIGHT STOP THANK AND PAY MISTER DODGE FOR HIS TROUBLE STOP WE ARE ALL ANXIOUS TO SEE YOU.   ARTHUR S. ALLEN"

He followed this with another cable:

PERCIVAL H. DODGE, AMERICAN CONSUL, COPENHAGEN, DENMARK. THANKS SO MUCH FOR YOUR KIND OFFICES IN REGARD TO MY SON STOP IT IS GREATLY APPRECIATED STOP SEND ME MEMORANDUM OF ANY EXPENSE. ARTHUR S. ALLEN."

From the Consul to Mr. Allen:

"MONEY RECEIVED STOP SON ARRIVING NEW YORK SEPTEMBER FOURTEENTH STOP FREDERICK EIGHT.   CONSUL WINSHIP."

SAGA OF *DIRECTION*

Under the date August 30, 1929, and carrying the letterhead of Charles D. Mower, Yacht Designer, City Island, New York, is the following:

CHARLES D. MOWER
YACHT DESIGNER
POWER YACHTS --- AUXILIARY CRUISERS
RACING YACHTS
CITY ISLAND
NEW YORK CITY
TELEPHONE 1423 CITY ISLAND

August 30, 1929.

Mr. Arthur F. Allen,
Philipse Manor, N.Y.

Dear Mr. Allen:-

It has been suggested to me that you might be interested in a position as draughtsman and, if so, I would be very glad to have you call on me for an interview.

I am connected with Henry B. Nevins, Inc and need an assistant on detail drawing work for the yard and on my personal designing. The close contact with actual construction work in the yard offers an unusual opportunity for gaining practical knowledge of yacht construction.

Please let me know if you are interested and I will be pleased to make an appointment.

Yours very truly,

Charles D Mower

128

Then, abruptly, there is a poetic obituary for Arthur S. Allen Jr. that appeared in a Tarrytown, N.Y., newspaper the day after his death.

This is followed by a cable from Rockwell Kent to Allen Sr.:

"KOBENHAVEN, SEPT. 24 1929 1:52 PM. KENTALLEN NY GREENLAND STYRELSE WILL PURCHASE BOAT STOP   ADVISE YOU GIVE ME AUTHORITY TO ACT FOR YOU STOP REPLY CARE STYRELSE.

ROCKWELL"

From this it is clear that Kent had learned of Sam's death by cable, and that this was his first response to that news. There is no cable of condolence from him in the scrapbook which is, I believe, 100 percent complete.

But, of all the letters of condolence in the scrapbook I shall quote only from that of Rockwell Kent. It is written on the personal stationery of Knud Rasmusen, the famous Greenland explorer, from Hundested, Denmark, where the Kents were visiting on October 2, 1929, and Kent was completing his illustrations for *Moby Dick*, which his wife, Frances, had brought with her across the Atlantic.

One of DIRECTON'S original deadeyes, recovered by Fred Pinaud at Baddeck, Nova Scotia, after the death of Arthur S. Allen Sr.

RASMUSSEN

HUNDESTED

October 2ᵈ 1929

Dear Arthur :—

Sam was as fine and brave a
boy as ever walked the earth, and infinitely
more than that — as you alone could know.
We can now do nothing but, knowing your
terrible sorrow, tell you that we love you;
and then, about his death, be silent.

Maybe I should not at this
time have intruded upon you with my
cable about the boat. It seemed to me,
however, important that you should be
given instant opportunity to alter those
arrangements about the boat which had
been made in anticipation of Sam's return
to Greenland — principally that you might
not become involved in unnecessary expense.
I had, on the day preceding my learning
of Sam's death, inspected and checked the
materials for the repairing of the boat,
which were assembled on the wharf for
shipment. The last steamer of this

130

October 2d, 1929
Hundested

Dear Arthur,

 Sam was as fine and brave a boy as ever walked the earth, and infinitely more than that—as you alone could know. We can do nothing about his death but, knowing your terrible sorrow, tell you that we love you; and then, about his death, be silent.

 Maybe I should not at this time have intruded upon you with my cable about the boat. It seemed to me, however, important that you should be given instant opportunity to alter those arrangements about the boat which had been made in anticipation of Sam's return to Greenland—principally that you might not become involved in unnecessary expense. I had, on the day preceding my learning of Sam's death, inspected and checked the materials for repairing the boat which were assembled on the wharf for shipment (to Greenland). The last steamer of the year sails tomorrow. If, as I thought likely, you wished to dispose of the wreck, this was the last opportunity for full instructions to be sent to Greenland. For if the Greenland Government had bought it, their repairs and alterations would have been of a different nature from those you intended. I immediately consulted the Director of the Gronlands Styrelse and received what I felt to be a most considerable offer to purchase the boat at a price named by two expert appraisers. I have given him now your cable rejecting the offer. He would appreciate your informing him, either through me or directly, what you intend to do with the boat.

 You see, Arthur, Sam owned the boat. (That was his statement at the enquiry.) I do not think that the Gronlands Styrelse will question your present title to it, or shall I say, require legal proof of it, but it is their right to be immediately informed of any change of plans such as the present emergency entails.

 You have not hinted what your intentions are. If you propose to send another crew for it by all means submit that proposal to the Gronlands Styrelse. You may not appreciate the difficulties of obtaining permission to visit Greenland. They are great and, I have come to know, properly so.

 If, by (the time of) the receipt of this letter, the materials for the boat have not left for Greenland, and you still wanted to keep the boat, I would have suggested that you have it brought to Copenhagen. I now think you could arrange to have the boat, after it has been repaired, sailed to Ivigtut, and from there brought to New York by steamer.

 It is my advice that you do not send Lucian Cary Jr. for it.

 In any case, please inform the Gronlands Styrelse what you intend to do.

 I am enclosing a letter to Lucian CARY (Senior) asking him to pay me what I advanced to his son. Won't you please add your request to mine—and please address and forward my letter? (REGISTERED, and keep the slip!)

 We are wonderfully situated here in a little house overlooking the sea on the west coast of Zeeland. I am hard at work. In Greenland I accomplished a great deal which you shall see in time.

 Our heartfelt sympathy to your family.
 Faithfully,
 Rockwell

131

*The model of DIRECTION made by
Mynart Ladd in 1932, showing the
rust streaks and barnacles with which
he decorated her hull. His widow,
Mrs. Myrick (Ginny) Freeman Jr.,
recovered the model and presented it
to the author in 1973. W. Perry
Curtiss, a modeler, restored it to
its original condition—without
disturbing the barnacles.*

ARTIFACTS & MEMORIES

In 1932, the late Mynart Ladd, then a student at Chesire Academy, Connecticut, where a brother of Arthur Allen Sr. was a faculty member, became fascinated by *Direction*. He built a handsome model of her from the plans which appeared in the endpapers of *Under Sail to Greenland*. Hoping to sell the model to Arthur S. Allen Sr., he took it to Allen's New York office. But Allen did not like the realistic barnacles with which Marty had decorated her bottom, nor the rust streaks running down from her chainplates. It was no sale; Marty found another buyer.

132

Forty years later, in 1972, Marty's widow, Ginny, re-acquired the model and presented it to me. It was in poor condition, but my neighbor, W. Perry Curtiss, did a beautiful job of restoring it.

Fred Pinaud, Walter Pinaud's son, went searching one day underneath a building at the Pinaud Yacht Yard in Baddeck, and after recovering it, presented me with one of *Direction's* deadeyes that had been replaced with a turnbuckle when she was changed over to a marconi rig years before. I have already mentioned that his father had given us the half-rotted nameboard carved by Rockwell Kent.

Like one hot coal keeping its neighbors aglow, all these bits and pieces fired me to furthur investigation. One night while reading over some of the old correspondence, I spotted one of Rockwell Kent's *Asgaard* letterheads and, just for the fun of it, wrote a letter to Mrs. Kent at that address, although I was not really sure there *was* a Mrs. Kent. I asked what had become of the movies I knew Kent had taken while *Direction* was pounding on the rocks in Greenland.

By return mail I received a letter that began, "Dear Mr. Vilas: I am taking the liberty of answering the letter you wrote, presumably to my widow." It was signed by Rockwell Kent! He advised me that the movies were in the mail to me. When I received the reel, I had it copied, and returned the original to Kent. (Some years later the original was destroyed when the Kent house was struck by lightning and burned. I was able to make a duplicate from my negative and send it to him.) There was more correspondence, plus the delightful weekend spent with the Kents at Ausable Forks, New York.

Let me tell you a bit about that memorable visit. Margaret and I arrived on a Saturday evening. We entered the Kent home to find over the mantel the magnificent painting of the Greenlandic girl as described in the section on Rockwell Kent. I am vague about other details of the room, so attention-demanding were our fascinating hosts, but I do remember in the background a concert grand Steinway. This indicated to me that some member of the family must be musical. Not since my own grandmother was living had I been in a private home containing a full size concert grand. I had a strong urge to try it out but managed to restrain myself.

We arrived at the proper moment for libations which were promptly served, and quite naturally we began to get acquainted through our common interest in *Direction*. It was not until after supper that we got down to serious business, and I opened up my tape recorder to preserve the visit for posterity. I produced *Direction's* log book with Kent's signature along with that of Allen and Cary. Kent had no recollection of ever signing it or having seen the log book before, but he was tremendously interested. There was much more that he had forgotten over the years, including the fact that he had carved *Direction's* nameboard. I quoted, however, from his letter of 1928 saying that he would do so.

Upon playing that tape back later on in my own home, I found it to be a bitter disappointment. I myself talked too much. I have been greatly annoyed by radio interviewers who monopolize a conversation with a distinguished celebrity, and here I was doing it myself. To inspire responses in him, I read aloud from the log and he managed to get a few precious words in edgewise. In describing the shipwreck he said that *Direction's* pounding on the rocks on her side while he was below decks salvaging gear and food, was so violent that the ceiling was ripped out, nails and all, and was falling on his head. His resentment over Lucian Cary (whom he dubbed "Cupid" throughout *N by E*) was as intense as if the incidents had happened only yesterday.

At breakfast the following morning Kent volunteered that the reason he had attended Architectural School at Columbia was that his parents did not consider a career as an artist respectable. Just as soon as he could establish himself as an artist, he did so. He also brought up the subject of communism. He denied most emphatically that he ever was a communist. He discussed his bout and victory with the State Department over obtaining a passport to visit the Soviet Union. While Kent's bright star reached its zenith in the United States, in the 1930's, in the Soviet Union his star shone brightly throughout his lifetime, and there he has remained a national hero. He and his wife Sally enjoyed many return engagements to Russia to be honored by Soviet officialdom and, incidently, to spend rubles he had earned there, but which could not be taken from the country.

In the United States Navy you must be dead before a destroyer can be named after you. Thus your record is known and no blemish of later behavior can mar the honor or the prestige of the Navy. Similarly in the art world no future misdemeanors can be committed against the establishment if you are no longer living. It is then safe to pile your name with kudos. The publication *Art World* in its issue for March 1977 lists simultaneously two prominent mid-town art galleries in Manhattan with exclusive Rockwell Kent exhibits. Price tags on some of the paintings exceed $20,000.00 and they are selling. What a contrast to Chanler Chapman's letter of 1924 in which he sneeringly comments of a Kent exhibit, "Not much financial success." Two books reproducing Kent art have been recently published; *The Prints of Rockwell Kent* by Dan Burne Jones, and the *Illustrations of Rockwell Kent* by Fridloff Johnson and John Gorton. Each has its individual merits with no overlap. Presently in preparation are two books about Kent, one a biography by David Stephen Traxel, backed by a research grant from the Smithsonian, and the other an anthology of Kent's literary and artistic work to be edited by Fridloff Johnson in collaboration with John F. H. Gorton.

Shortly after we delivered *Direction* to Connecticut from Nova Scotia in 1946, I received a letter from Winthrop Warner, the naval architect. In it he told me of the Reverend Lewis H. Davis, then minister of the Methodist church in Bristol, Connecticut. Mr. Davi had blueprints of *Direction's* plans and would be happy to give them to me if I were interested. We arranged for an excursion aboard *Direction* with Mr. Davis, his wife, Helen, and their daughters. He arrived with the blueprints under his arm and departed, leaving them aboard *Direction* for us to keep, and eventually enter into the pages of this book.

It seems that Mr. Davis had arranged with Mr. Allen to charter *Direction* for an extended cruise in the West Indies, but eventually purchased a different boat in which he was wrecked off the coast of Cuba. However, he had borrowed the plans and was unable to return them until after Mr. Allen's death in 1945.

This was the beginning of my remarkable collection of memorabilia and artifacts which was followed soon after by the papers and documents from Peggy and Harry Calnan. The Davises now live in their retirement home on Shelter Island, New York, and we still visit them when we are in the neighborhood.

One artifact not in my study is the unbelievably heavy standing rigging that held up *Direction's* telegraph pole of a mast. It still remains in the shop at Pinaud's yard in Baddeck, and in conjunction with the yard crane is used from time to time for lifting heavy objects. The eyes at the ends of the wire are not even spliced; they are seized with marlin, thereby doubling their ⅝-inch diameter. No wonder the boat was topheavy!

The magpie or pack rat impulse in me has been fostered by the tendency of others who, sharing my interest, unload on me oddments from *Direction* for which they have no room but value too much to throw away. That collecting these memorabilia has become an obsession, I would not deny, but it has been a satisfying obsession that has added much to the pleasure of owning *Direction*.

PART IV:

Direction
Today

M.V.P.V.

A CRUISING PHILOSOPHY

AUTHOR'S NOTE: When Murray Davis was launching his new magazine Cruising World, *he asked me to write an article for his first issue. It was to be a philosophical piece explaining what cruising is all about and what makes us "cruising types" tick. I was delighted with the assignment since from many years' experience I had reached the conclusion that the last thing editors of the yachting magazines wanted in their pages was philosophy.*

The first article was originally called "From Here To There With Nothing But The Wind," and appeared in the Fall 1974 issue of Cruising World. *The second one was entitled "The Cruising Committment," and was printed in the February 1975 issue of the same magazine.*

They are included in this section, partly to explain myself, partly to describe the kind of cruising life I've led for the past half century. Perhaps you'll find that it hasn't changed that much today, after all.

*With wings to roam the earth,
DIRECTION has released us
from the bondage of civilization.*

WHAT MAKES US TICK
(1974)

MAN WAS BORN TO BE FREE. It is contrary to his nature to remain fettered to mundane jobs. The more complex and sophisticated the civilization in which he finds himself, the greater is the conflict between the lure of material and social amenities, and the urge to break away from it all. Our caveman instincts lie just beneath the surface, beckoning us to the mountaintop, the forest, or the sea. But our skins are thin; our bodies fragile. We have no wings with which to fly; no well-oiled feathers to protect us from the elements. For too many eons have we been made soft by the comfort of heated homes and cooked meals.

In spite of this, some people have found the means to take wing and fly away. In the dim past, man invented the boat, and eventually developed the ship. He became free to roam the face of the earth in search of whale oil, silks, spices, plunder or other forms of material gain. Today's civilization hardly permits a man to earn a living roaming the seas in a small boat. Even the independent fisherman is being phased out by stern trawlers and huge factory ships.

So, to keep his spirit from withering, man has had to invent the yacht—the cruising sailing yacht. In place of the wings he lacks, he has sails to take him anywhere. In place of feathers, blubber or fur he has decks to shelter him from the elements. Thus can he roam the world with the freedom of whales or birds. Although his yacht may never leave the confines of San Francisco Bay or Long Island Sound, the potential is there and the dream is sustained to help soften the harshness of a crowded, competitive existence he has not the courage to forsake.

How else can one explain today's proliferation of the small, family cruising yacht, or justify crowding one's wife and children into the confines of a 23-foot sloop or catboat while a spacious apartment or comfortable suburban home remains empty and deserted every summer weekend and vacation period?

How, except that such a choice allows us to savor more deeply the sweet nectars that this world has to offer—the freshness of a pre-dawn morning, the mystery of a moonlit night, the thrill of being carried from here to there by nothing but the winds that God provides? Until you have cruised, you have only been half alive. Such, at least, is the conceit of those of us who embrace this life. Those who have not experienced it can never understand completely what I am talking about. It's like trying to describe a rainbow to a person blind from birth.

An older brother of mine first introduced me to cruising in his Wilton Crosby catboat more than half a century ago. Unfortunately, he only kept his boat for two years before he became hooked on respectability, and sold it. He put his freedom in hock to hold down a prestigious big-city job with adequate salary to support a proper home and raise a family.

In my case, once having tasted the joys of cruising, I became hooked the other way, so that my job and livelihood became secondary to my weekend cruising and all-too-brief vacations. When affluence eventually permitted it, my brother came back into yachting with all the spit and polish of the successful executive. After many years, when my own income permitted, I moved into a semi-respectable home, but never, for the past 50 years, have I been without a cruising sailboat.

Nancy Lee was my first "yacht," purchased in 1926 for $250. What did not show on the bill of sale was the franchise that came with her: cruising rights to the entire Atlantic seaboard. For all practical purposes I owned Hamburg Cove, the sand holes at Eatons Neck and Lloyd Neck, the Navesink River, and all of Narragansett and Chesapeake Bays—to say nothing of the Potomac River, Lake Champlain and Cuttyhunk Island. What is more, I did not have to pay any taxes. In exchange for that immunity, I happily shared my domains with the few other yachtsmen who sailed those waters in the 1920's and 1930's.

Nancy Lee was a 20-foot-keel catboat. Her iron shoe weighed 1200 pounds. She had a bowsprit and set a very small jib which, on occasion, could be run up on a shroud to serve as a storm trisail. Her accommodations consisted of two bunks with full sitting head room, a porcelain bucket for a head, a single-burner Primus stove for cooking, and a five-gallon crock to hold drinking water. I owned her for 20 years and during that time I acquired a wife and daughter.

NANCY LEE. Our 20-foot keel catboat anchored in the Hudson River, just below Albany. Owning her gave us title to "the entire Eastern seaboard."

Her sparse accommodations were entirely adequate for the needs of my youth. *Nancy Lee* was a very able vessel; none of this spade-rudder, fin-keel, light-displacement stuff. You could run her aground (and I frequently did) without doing permanent damage. Her three-and-a-half-foot draft meant that once aground you could always get out and push (and I frequently did that, too). She had an engine. It was a one-cylinder, four-and-a-half-horsepower Lathrop with what was known as a "make-and-break" ignition. It was such a simple affair that I prided myself on being able to disassemble it into its component parts, clean the ignition points, remove carbon from the piston and cylinder walls, and get it back together and running all in a single afternoon.

With the overlong boom of the catboat rig, plus her 1896 launching date, *Nancy Lee* was not exactly a boat in which to go to sea. But who cares? With her khaki sails for wings, and her canvas decks for shelter she made it possible for us to explore enough virgin cruising territory to consume our available time easily. We could enter gunkholes no longer accessible to us today with our present deep-draft, high-masted vessel.

What was nice about *Nancy Lee* was the casualness with which things could be accomplished. It was nothing to remove her mast at Troy, New York, on the Barge Canal, and restep it at Whitehall, New York, for a two weeks exploration of Lake Champlain, or to invite an overweight fisherman to sit on her bowsprit to depress the mast three inches for passage underneath the railway bridge at Canoe Place inlet for a cruise on Moriches and Great South Bays, Long Island.

The Delaware-Raritan Canal was still in operation in the 1920's, so Chesapeake Bay could be reached by small cruising boats without their having to run the Jersey coast outside in the Atlantic to Cape May. By means of the Canal, we once spent a night, of all places, in Princeton, New Jersey. The next day, with no advance notice that we were to become airborne, we suddenly looked down from our decks to discover that we were sailing over what looked like an ancient Roman aqueduct with a freight train passing beneath us on the Pennsylvania Railroad tracks! You simply can't have experiences like that if you play golf or go to the track on Saturday afternoon.

*NANCY LEE locking through the
Delaware-Raritan Canal, the "inside"
route from New Jersey to Chesapeake Bay,
a canal now long closed, 1928*

When you own a boat, no matter how tiny, you make friends. Most of those friends are sailors. And if you are young, older friends like to have you along as an able hand. That is how my wife and I became friends with Robert and Dorothy Byerly. Like me, Bob Byerly did not change boats very often. His first was a flush-deck deep-draft cutter named *Owl*. She never had an engine nor did his second (and last) boat, the 45-foot flush-decked schooner *Owl II*. Yet Nova Scotia, Bermuda, and Newfoundland were as familiar to him as Lake Champlain and Long Island Sound were to us.

Cruising aboard *Owl II* with the Byerlys broadened our horizons extensively. I consider myself fortunate in being exposed to one of the very last of the pure sailing yachts, learning the techniques of handling one, and experiencing the joys of actually going to sea and sailing offshore.

145

Robert Byerly's schooner, OWL II, awaits a dawn breeze off Cutler, Maine. "She served to broaden our horizons beyond the scope of our little catboat."

With *Nancy Lee* resting on her home mooring, we would board the State of Maine Express to go Down East and cruise Penobscot Bay on *Owl II*, or put to sea for Atlantic Highlands via Nantucket Lightship. On one of these cruises between Maine and New Jersey we came within earshot of the diaphone on Nantucket Lightship in a pea soup fog with nothing but our "Dipsy" (deep-sea lead) and compass for navigation.

We beat down the channel between Georges Bank and Nantucket Shoals, and came about only when the lead line showed we were over either one. Taking a sounding was a 20-minute operation—while hove-to with the foresail aback. Having no engine, we of course had no electricity nor any modern aid to navigation.

If you are fortunate in buying the right boat to begin with, I see no reason for feeding brokerage fees to the trade by changing boats every other year—as so many of my friends seem to do. However, with our seven-year-old daughter not growing any smaller, and our 50-year-old catboat not growing any younger, we finally began to think of buying another boat, disloyal as it seemed to our beloved *Nancy Lee*.

If our first boat had served us for 20 years, we wondered, could we find another that would last the next 20 years?

146

Direction turned out to be the answer. With all the improvements and innovations we have added, I'd hate to change again and have to start over, once more installing the many labor-saving and comfort-giving devices that the naval architects manage to ignore in the so-called "modern" yacht.

For the first 20 years that we owned *Direction* she served as our weekend cottage and vacation hideaway. Except for sailing her home from Cape Breton Island where we purchased her, we never cruised east of Cape Cod. My New England conscience bound me to a job with too short a vacation. But Nantucket, the Elizabeth Islands and Martha's Vineyard were plenty to keep me and my family satisfied.

A favorite weekend hideaway for us used to be the Salmon River, which empties into the Connecticut River a mile above the East Haddam swing bridge. Until 1973 when the government revised it, Chart no. 266 showed no soundings whatsoever in the Salmon River. For this reason it remained an exclusive anchorage for us. I first sailed in there in my brother's Crosby catboat in 1924. In *Direction*, drawing 6'6", we moored bow and stern as there was no swinging room in the narrow deep-water channel to allow for the reversal of tidal currents.

Half a mile above the narrow entrance, the river opens up into a delightful basin a mile long by three eights of a mile wide. At the head is Mount Tom, and far beneath it lies a fault that is the source of seismic rumblings which made it a shrine for the Indian god, Machimoodus. The stream to the right of Mount Tom is the Moodus River, and the village lying at its headwaters is named Moodus.

A 17th-century burial ground lies back in the woods behind the next point above Cone Point on the chart, and the stream that tumbles down from a nearby waterfall had a mill on it in colonial days. Some of the cast-iron gears from its waterwheel lie in my garage today, awaiting the appropriate occasion to present them to an appreciative historical society.

Through the years, I came to consider that I owned the Salmon River. Canoeists from Elm Camp, later known as Ted Hilton's Vacation Hideaway, lying several miles upstream, were always so enslaved by the dinner bell that their time would run out just when they reached our anchorage, and they would have to hasten back for the next meal. As a result we rarely had "company" stay for any length of time, and never had to share our spot with other vessels, except those of our own invited friends.

147

But then came the crunch! Without so much as a by-your-leave, somebody plunked an atomic power plant right down on what I considered my private property! They cut swaths through the woods a few feet upstream from our anchorage, and strung high-tension wires across *my* beloved Salmon River! That taught me the folly of not obtaining title and paying taxes. That is why in 1965 I purchased a tract of waterfront land on the Bras d'Or Lakes of Cape Breton Island, to begin all over again.

This time I have a title and gladly pay my taxes. I have an anchorage with a mail box on shore, *Direction* serves as our floating home, and nobody is likely to erect an atomic power plant on the site during my lifetime. *Our* bald eagles sit on a treetop, gazing down on our cockpit while we sip our evening cocktails, a woodcock utters his fluttering cry as he dives toward his mate in a nearby field, and all is serene.

In fairness to the Connecticut Yankee Power Company of East Haddam, Connecticut, let me add that last fall, in a fit of nostalgia, I launched my canoe at the State Ramp just below the Salmon River entrance, and paddled up to my old haunts of a half a century ago. Except for the overhead wires, very little has changed, and the river remains largely unspoiled. I climbed my favorite hill, rested for half an hour under the towering conifers and recalled the days in the 1920's when I used to sit on the exact same spot, gazing down admiringly on *Nancy Lee*, lying at anchor beneath my feet.

The late Fessenden Blanchard and his wife, Mary, once spent a weekend with us aboard *Direction* on the Salmon River. Fes was under oath not to publicize the spot in his *Cruising Guide to the New England Coast.* But now that *Direction* is based more than 1000 miles away, and the government has finally printed the river's soundings on the chart, I am happy to tip you off.

Since the channel is unmarked, you had better plan your first arrival at close to low water so the mud banks can show you just where it lies. Deep water is obvious as far as the 15-foot sounding at the island labeled *Grass.* Anchor temporarily here. Then with your dinghy, stake out the channel as much farther as you care to go. You can easily carry 6'6" beyond the high-tension wires to where the eight-foot sounding on the chart marks the end of the deep channel. You can carry three feet of water—with care—up to where the channel deepens again with 11-, 7-, 17-, 9- and 7-foot soundings on the chart.

Dave Bacon's schooner, TERRY, and DIRECTION, moored stern to stern in the Salmon River. Each boat, with an anchor out ahead, is prepared to stem the tide whichever way it runs.

You can swing to an anchor up here beneath *my* towering pines, but lower down you must moor bow and stern. Our favorite spot for *Direction* was between the 9- and 7-foot soundings, just below the high-tension wires. Here you may enjoy the privacy and illusion of a lake in northern Maine while practically within commuting distance of New York City.

Nature has decreed that all forms of life shall multiply until some outside force brings further propagation to a halt. Spectacle Island on the Bras d'Or Lakes near Baddeck encapsulates this law. It is a small island, well offshore, once studded with tall black spruce trees. Some years ago an individualistic and imaginative cormorant forsook the crowded rookery of its birth and nested in one of these trees. No foxes or wildcats could swim out to prey on its young.

The cormorant's progeny thrived and returned next season to build more nests. Before anyone realized what was happening, the first nonhuman high-rise condominium came into existence. Today there are several dozen nests per tree, and originally there were more than 100 trees.

149

For 10 years we have been watching the progress of this community. The acid cormorant droppings have fouled the soil and killed the trees. Winter gales have blown the weaker trees down, and in a few more years Spectacle Island will have become a desert, no longer habitable. To draw a parallel between this island with its cormorants and our earth with its humans is irresistable. Like the island our earth is finite. Like the cormorants we are multiplying and fouling our habitat through sheer numbers, which are no longer checked by plagues or infant mortality.

I do not share, however, the righteous moral indignation of our ecologists. If, like the cormorants, we insist upon propagating to the saturation point, what more can we expect? But like the first enterprising cormorant who escaped the pressures of the rookery of its birth, I, too, have sought my own nesting site, far from the multiplying multitudes. Like the cormorant I could never have done so without my wings with which to fly and my well-oiled feathers to shelter me.

The wings may be dacron cloth, the feathers mere wood or fiberglass, but the end result is the same. Crowded by the pressures of civilization I have flown to a new nesting site. If you are the owner of a cruising yacht, you can fly, too. At any time you may take wing. But even if you don't, the knowledge that you could, should sustain your spirit until the moment finally arrives for you to sail off and attain your Nirvana.

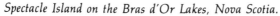

Spectacle Island on the Bras d'Or Lakes, Nova Scotia.

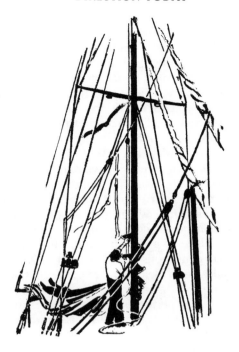

THE CRUISING COMMITMENT
(1975)

RARE IS THE MAN with total commitment to the cruising life. Rare, too, is the man who, once tasting that life, does not dream of a total commitment to it for some time in the future. There are even cruising clubs which demand a degree of commitment from their members.

To qualify for membership in the Seven Seas Cruising Assn., for instance, a candidate must live aboard his boat at least six months of the year. The Ocean Cruising Club requires that a candidate must have made an ocean passage of 1000 miles or more. How many gainfully occupied persons with family responsibilities can meet these standards? It is surprising that there are enough so that each organization thrives; but for the vast majority of people such commitment is nearly impossible.

Nevertheless, the rewards of the cruising life are directly proportional to the degree of commitment a person is able or willing to give. We are all oriented to land living, and indoctrinated with the work ethic, slaves to the clock and calendar. The experienced cruising man learns to be ruled by the tides and the wind. And there lies the basic conflict. How wisely you resolve it has an important bearing on how much you get out of cruising.

Most of us are vacation and weekend cruisers. We find our lives divided into two opposing but balancing units. Monday through Friday we live by the work ethic, 9:00 to 5:00, with a lunch hour and two coffee breaks. On weekends we become free. Or do we?

Most certainly not if we insist on bringing our work ethic with us. Man is a creature of habit, and it is not easy to throw off the practice of clock-watching when you step aboard your boat. Many a weekend can be spoiled because you promise or resolve to get to a certain place at a certain time, only to discover when the day comes that conditions are such that sailing in the opposite direction would be a pleasure, but to keep the appointment is an endurance contest.

The first thing the experienced cruising person learns is not to make those appointments, even if his land-oriented friends cannot understand his reluctance to be committed to their schedules. They simply don't realize that boats are not like automobiles.

If he dwells and works in a large city, the next thing he learns is to base his boat as far away as possible, doing his traveling by car, plane or train. Then, once he steps aboard he does not have that urge to make haste and get away. He is there and away already. Then should tide and wind serve, he may set sail in the late evening and drift a mile or two to a quiet anchorage; if not, he can be happy at his slip or mooring. I wonder how many times through the years I have done exactly that.

From my home in New Haven, I would often drive the 30 miles to Essex, Connecticut, on a Friday evening after work and board *Direction* at the Essex Yacht Club. I might have arrived just as the afternoon southerly was petering out, set sail, dropped the mooring and drifted on a rising tide two miles up stream to Hamburg Cove to anchor and get a quiet night's sleep.

Or it might be that I arrived at the top of the tide with a moonlit night in prospect and a flat calm. I might have then elected to ride the ebb under power downriver and out to Long Island Sound, anchoring before midnight in West Harbor on Fisher's

Island, all poised for a sail to Block Island the next day. None of this, mind you, would be planned ahead but, according to the conditions I found upon arrival, I might go one way or the other.

My wife and I learned this trick fairly early in the game when, as newlyweds, we were Manhattan apartment-dwellers. We based our catboat *Nancy Lee* at the American Yacht Club, 30 miles away in Rye, New York. We would get there regularly on a Friday evening, step aboard and then decide whether to remain on our mooring, which was pleasant enough, or, if there was a breeze, sail around into the lee of nearby Hen Island for the night, or, if a southwest wind showed signs of holding, sail off to the eastward, perhaps to the "sand hole" at Lloyd Neck before midnight. But at no time did we ever say, "Come hell or high water, we'll be at such and such a place at such and such a time."

What I am trying to drive home is the kind of commitment that I believe produces the most satisfaction when cruising. Once you step aboard, even for a weekend, *commit yourself to the life as though you were living aboard year round!* The contrast with your other, land existence will make both more rewarding.

The same idea applies to that vacation cruise you've been dreaming about all year. Don't plan to sail great distances in a limited time unless the winds and tides give you a lucky break. This applies particularly if you have children aboard. They need beaches to swim from, and islands to explore. Save all that aggressiveness for your job, where it will earn you money—and promotions.

So far we have only considered the man with a minimum commitment—the vacation-weekend cruiser. Except in our dreams, this is the category in which most of us find ourselves—a compromise, but a happy one. Our jobs are more fun because of our sailing and each contributes to the zest of living.

But what about the Eric Hiscocks, the Miles Smeetons and countless others whose commitment approaches totality? If you have no other home but your boat and spend your life circling the globe then your commitment is 100 percent. But is it? I understand that the Smeetons have sold *Tzu Hang* and settled on a farm miles inland in British Columbia. They have retired from cruising at a time when many people retire to go cruising.

I hear that the Hiscocks are considering doing the same, after just one more circumnavigation. Their commitment has been total but short lived. In my case, my commitment has been partial but has lasted more than half a century.

Although you may dream of emulating the Hiscocks or the Smeetons, the chances are that your commitment will be closer to mine, and, to be fair, working for a living and assuming civic responsibilities are not all that bad.

But perhaps your youngest child has just graduated from college, your mortgage is all paid up, and a new company policy has made your job so distasteful that you are ready for a change. Perhaps *then* is the time to take a year or two off, circle the globe or visit the South Sea Islands; and then return to a less-demanding job and fewer responsibilities.

Many young couples have also followed this dream even when encumbered with family responsibilities. Wayne and Chris Carpenter of San Diego dropped anchor near us on the Bras d'Or Lakes in 1973 with their double-ender, *Marie Rose.* Time ran out on their way south so they wintered at Mahone Bay, Nova Scotia, aboard their boat which was frozen in ice. The children attended the local schools while Chris took a job as draftsman, and Wayne wrote press releases for Paceship, Ltd.

I visited them in March 1974 and can vouch for the happy and adventurous existence they were leading. Theirs was most certainly total commitment. I last heard from them by postcard mailed from Madeira in July 1975. I have no doubt that in a few years Wayne will return to San Diego and resume his career as a newspaper man, with his commitment to cruising reduced to more manageable proportions. Meanwhile, the entire family is having the adventure of a lifetime. *(My guess was right. In early 1977 I learned that Wayne had sold his boat and was working as editor of* Pacific Skipper *in San Diego.)*

Relatively few of us are willing to make such commitments as the Carpenters, the Smeetons or the Hiscocks. But there are many stages—intermediate stages—in which to find your niche. The more the commitment, the greater the reward, but at the same time the greater the sacrifice. So if you must dream, it might be wise to temper your dreams with that realization—and then your cruising life may provide the fulfillment you seek.

(Photo on next page):
*DIRECTION with
her present-day rig,
showing the triple
roller-furling
headsails.*

154

DIRECTION'S DETAILS

AUTHOR'S NOTE: The setting sun has just broken out from under the overcast, throwing long shadows across our anchorage. Take your glass and come on deck so that we can look over my accumulation of what the late Ham de Fontaine might have called "gadgets and gilhickies." These are the additions, modifications and improvements I have made to Direction *over the years.*

Much of what follows describes changes to a boat that took years to work out through slow germination, until my conservative mind—and cautious action—saw a way to solve each problem. In the three decades I have owned this cutter, some of my friends have run through five or six boats, learning the new ones all over again, adapting to each new one's eccentricities and then—all too soon it often seemed to me—moving on to yet another.

I could not comfortably have followed that pattern. It took so long to make Direction *"just right" that after five years of ownership I could not have faced the switch to a new boat and getting to know her and solve her problems all over again. I have never regretted staying with* Direction; *she suits us, and we trust her.*

Let's begin with an article I wrote for Sail *magazine in August 1973, one that described how I turned* Direction *into what I call "a singlehander for geriatrics."*

155

ON TRIPLE ROLLER-FURLING HEADSAILS
(1973)

drawings by Margaret van Pelt Vilas

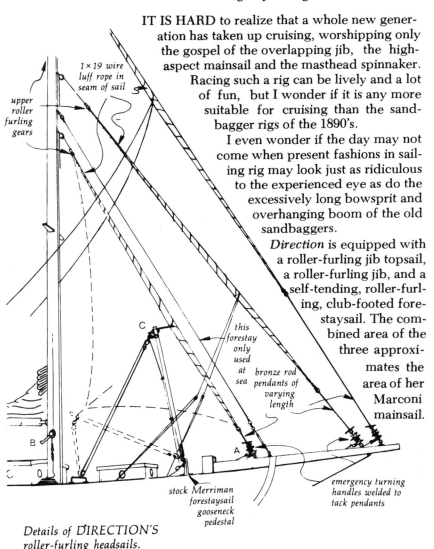

IT IS HARD to realize that a whole new generation has taken up cruising, worshipping only the gospel of the overlapping jib, the high-aspect mainsail and the masthead spinnaker. Racing such a rig can be lively and a lot of fun, but I wonder if it is any more suitable for cruising than the sandbagger rigs of the 1890's.

I even wonder if the day may not come when present fashions in sailing rig may look just as ridiculous to the experienced eye as do the excessively long bowsprit and overhanging boom of the old sandbaggers.

Direction is equipped with a roller-furling jib topsail, a roller-furling jib, and a self-tending, roller-furling, club-footed forestaysail. The combined area of the three approximates the area of her Marconi mainsail.

1 × 19 wire luff rope in seam of sail

upper roller furling gears

this forestay only used at sea

bronze rod pendants of varying length

C

B

A

stock Merriman forestaysail gooseneck pedestal

emergency turning handles welded to tack pendants

Details of DIRECTION'S roller-furling headsails.

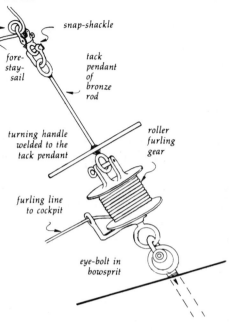

snap-shackle

fore-
stay-
sail

tack
pendant
of
bronze
rod

turning handle
welded to the
tack pendant

roller
furling
gear

furling line
to cockpit

eye-bolt in
bowsprit

This means that I can halve her total sail area merely by pulling three "strings" from the cockpit.

The three roller-furling gears have been in constant use for more than 20 years, with only two minor failures. I have cruised the waters of Long Island Sound, Nova Scotia and Newfoundland with complete confidence in the safety and reliability of the rig.

In fact, I consider the hazards of the roller-furling gear, implied or real, to be far outweighed by the dangers of going forward in a seaway to furl headsails while hanging on to a plunging bowsprit or pulpit. This is especially true if you cruise short-handed or singlehanded as I frequently do.

The three headsails are set on Wyckham-Martin No. 3 roller-furling gears. Twenty-five years ago, when I began installing the gears one by one, the Wyckham-Martins were the only gears that did not have enclosed drums and did not require the use of wire on the spool.

Because I was among the early yachtsmen on this side of the Atlantic to try out roller-furling gears, I had no one either to lead or mislead me in their installation. I had to figure it all out myself— perhaps a lucky happenstance considering some present-day installations.

My first problem was the pendants holding the tack of the jibs down to the bowsprit on a cutter whose rig had been designed more than a century ago. The original pendants were of manila and hardly satisfactory for a roller-furling system. Even wire rope might come unlaid when transferring the torsion of the gear to the sail.

To solve the problem, I substituted bronze rods with eyes brazed on each end. The rod for the topsail was 12 feet long, for the jib two feet long, and for the staysail 10 inches long. I also had short

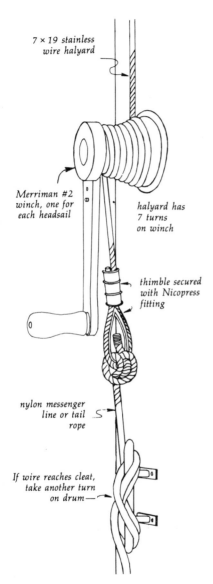

7 x 19 *stainless wire halyard*

Merriman #2 *winch, one for each headsail*

halyard has 7 turns on winch

thimble secured with Nicropress fitting

nylon messenger line or tail rope

If wire reaches cleat, take another turn on drum—

pieces of rod brazed to these bronze "pendants" at right angles, to enable me to wind up the sails by hand should the line at the furling drum foul or break.

The jibs were secured to the halyards and bronze-rod pendants with snap shackles. I also made up wires with thimbles on both ends the same length as the luff ropes of the sails, so that in case of a hurricane I could quickly unshackle the rolled-up sails and substitute the wires to reduce windage and the risk of damaging the sails.

The one-part halyards are 7 x 19 stainless steel wire, and the thimbles on both ends are fastened with Nicropress fittings rather than splices, which might fail were torsion to unlay the wire.

These halyards pass through blocks on the mast and lead down to No. 2 Merriman winches where seven turns are taken around the drums. Rope tails of ⅜-inch dacron are tied to the lower thimbles of the halyards. With no strain, because of the seven turns of wire, the light dacron is adequate for cleating to the mast and for lowering the rolled-up sails. An important feature of this rig is the single-part halyard. In my opinion, a two-part halyard would present a serious hazard.

More than one skipper has had the experience of fouling the wire in an enclosed furling drum, and then, in a bit of panic, lowering the half-furled sail and having the torsion twist and jam the two-part halyard when the sail is part way down. The wind always seems to be piping up when this happens, and the half-lowered jib unrolls and takes charge, leaving the skipper in real trouble.

158

To eliminate this difficulty, most roller-furling rigs have a fitting attached to the halyard block at the head of the jib. This fitting rides on a fixed forestay set forward of the jib and prevents the two-part halyard from twisting as it is lowered. This helps to keep the halyard from twisting, but when, sailing off the wind, an experienced crew may roll up this stay inside the sail, especially if the sail and stay are set close to each other. I feel strongly that the only foolproof system of roller-furling for boats under 40 feet is to use a single-part halyard heavy enough to take the load, and a sheave of proper diameter in the block to take the size of wire.

The line that winds up on the roller-furling drum is ¼-inch dacron. If I cannot break the line with my hands, it is strong enough for any pull I might make in furling the sail, and it is much easier on the hands than wire. Should it break, a thing which has never happened to me, I could go forward and wind up the sail with the bronze "handle," mentioned earlier.

A wire with a rope tail tends to foul every fairlead, stanchion and deck fitting as it travels along the deck. Wire loosely wound on an enclosed drum often gets hopelessly fouled just where it can't be untangled. I've become convinced that simple dacron line wound around an open, accessible drum is the best arrangement.

If proper tension is not maintained on the line as the sail is unfurled, the coil gets larger on the drum until a loose loop slips off and takes a turn around the drum fittings. When this happens, I go forward and wind the sail up with the bronze "handle" until I have enough slack to clear the tangle.

My self-tending, roller-furling, club-forestaysail is unique. Stafford Johnson once asked a well-known sailmaker if he would make him a roller-furling club-footed staysail. The sailmaker said quite firmly, "Impossible. You can't make such a thing."

"Don't tell me that!" Stafford exclaimed, "I have just been cruising with one."

In certain respects, the sailmaker's reaction was justified. I confess that I could not work out the device on paper. Instead, I had the roller-furling forestaysail made up, and installed it loose-footed. I then measured the vertical distance from the rolled-up clew to the deck. I next measured the horizontal distance from the unrolled clew to its intersection with the vertical line. This distance determined the length of the club, which was 14 inches less than the vertical dimension. I then ordered a 14-inch-high Merriman pedestal gooseneck, a stock item.

The pedestal gooseneck plus the club made a perfect fit from deck to clew with sail furled. The club also just cleared the mast when the sail was unfurled. To get proper lead for the clew pendant (or staysail outhaul), the club must extend well beyond the clew.

I spliced a short length of half-inch Dacron to the clew. This clew line leads down through the outer of two holes drilled through the end of the club, then back up through the inner hole, then around again through the loop between the two holes. Like a clove hitch on a post, its own pressure holds it in place and, like adjusting a clove hitch, I can easily alter its length. Once it is set properly, I marl-hitch the leftover line to the club, just to keep it out of the way.

If the staysail is dry and the sheet is slack, the sail rolls up perfectly in spite of the arc described by the club in its travel from horizontal to the vertical position. If the sail is wet or is rolled up before a strong following wind, the furl may be messy, but, nevertheless, it is a furl.

On conventional roller-furled jibs, the lead of the sheet bisects the miter of the sail and the jib rolls tightly and evenly. However, with the increased tension on the foot created by the angle of the clew line when nearly furled, my staysail furl may be a bit messy with a tight foot and loose leech. If I get such a bad furl, I ignore it until I am at anchor, at which time I can reroll the sail into a neater harbor furl.

To control the notorious tendency of roller jibs to sag off to leeward, I tighten up my running backstay with the help of a deck winch. Boats with tight permanent backstays don't have this problem.

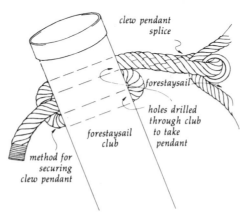

clew pendant
splice

forestaysail

holes drilled
through club
to take
pendant

forestaysail
club

method for
securing
clew pendant

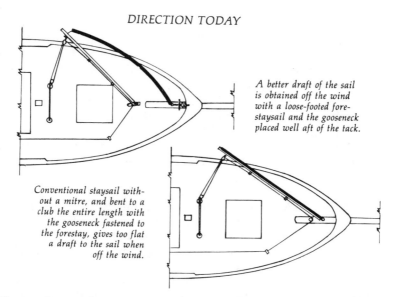

A better draft of the sail is obtained off the wind with a loose-footed fore-staysail and the gooseneck placed well aft of the tack.

Conventional staysail without a mitre, and bent to a club the entire length with the gooseneck fastened to the forestay, gives too flat a draft to the sail when off the wind.

When sailing off the wind, the forestaysail behaves as if it had no club at all, because of the position of the gooseneck well aft of the tack. The sail achieves a much better draft off the wind than a conventional staysail, where the sail is bent to the club, and the club secured to the forestay.

So much for the details of the rig. But how does she sail? Without an overlapping headsail, I do not get the slot effect one gets with a genoa. Performance with a number two or even a number three genoa would be much better. However, once I unfurl the jib, it is simply amazing how this heavy old boat picks up her skirts and moves! And when the jib topsail is set, wow! With all the talk about leading edges, just look at what she has. And slots! The boat has enough to keep any aerodynamics expert happy.

I have often been tempted to borrow a masthead genoa to set in place of my jib topsail—just to see what would happen. Brad Ripley did this on his Rhodes double-ender, *Wagtail*, and promptly cleaned up in Off Soundings Club racing. But I would lose too much of my cruising advantage, so I only dream of that idea.

You have to sail with this rig to appreciate what it does for the singlehander. True, to tack I have to scramble a bit to handle two sheets. But the staysail is self-tending on a traveler, and the running backstays are both set up when close hauled, hence neither needs tending, leaving only the jib and topsail to be cast off and sheeted down again. My technique is to get the jib around as the

161

boat luffs, leaving the topsail aback until I have cleated the jib sheet. Then I release the weather topsail sheet and scurry to cleat the leeward sheet before the wind fills the sail and makes it too hard to handle.

For short tacking, I roll up the two outer jibs and convert my boat into a knockabout, relaxing in the cockpit with nothing to do but flip the tiller over. If there is promise of a longer leg, I unroll the jib or even the topsail for a while, knowing full well that as soon as I come to the next short leg it will be no effort at all to roll them up again.

For Long Island Sound sailing, I removed my original fore-stay as it was too close to the staysail and was apt to be rolled up in the sail. That left no forward support for the mast but the three roller-furling rigs. When later I took the boat to sea, I fitted a new permanent forestay with an eight-inch clearance and never rolled it up in the sail again. I put standard plastic chafing tubes on this stay to prevent wear on the jib sheets when tacking. The topsail sheets rub against the luff of the jib which is reinforced.

There never is any need to reef a headsail. The foretriangle is already broken up into three nearly equal increments. Should it come on to blow, the first thing I do is tie a very deep reef in the mainsail instead of rolling up any headsails. I do not have roller-reefing gear on the main boom because that would mean sacrific-ing my gallows frame and inboard mainsheet, both of which I consider more important.

If the wind pipes up still more, I roll the jibtopsail first, and next the jib. If the wind lightens, I can unroll them with no effort, and then roll them up again if the lull is merely temporary.

Under deep-reefed main and forestaysail, I have a well-balanced knockabout rig, comfortable in winds over 30 knots and safe in blows to 40. However, if there is any build-up of seas, a Colin Archer-design with her deep forefoot and full body forward, may hobbyhorse. If, under these conditions, I have to go to weather, I turn on the engine and motorsail. In the protected waters of the Bras d'Or Lakes, where most of my daysailing is now done, I rarely have to do this as the boat sails quickly and comfortably in any kind of wind.

I am currently conducting a test between canvas and Dacron to see whether water rot or sun rot gets one or the other first. The jib is made of khaki duck and the forestaysail and topsail of maroon terelene (Dacron). Another few years should prove which is the more durable when left out in summer sun and rain.

INTERNAL BALLAST

IF YOU COMPARE the earliest photographs of *Direction* with contemporary ones, you will notice that right after her launching she sat high on the water with the freeboard of a Tahiti ketch, and had quite an angle of heel under sail, even when the wind hardly rippled the water. In more recent pictures, she looks like an altogether different boat. She seems to be much longer because she shows less freeboard, and what is more important, she obviously stands up to a breeze of wind.

Moses Bartlett in Battle Harbour, Labrador, was the first one to comment on her being too heavily rigged and too lightly ballasted. In fact, she had no inside ballast. Rockwell Kent made the same complaint in private, although he did it tactfully; he did not say it for publication. Edward L. Ayres made the same comment again in his log of 1932, but it went unheeded along with his many other sound recommendations. By the time I got *Direction* in 1946, something had been done about it. Her bilge and the space under her starboard transoms were filled with rusty iron in the form of a few 75-pound pigs and a lot of scrap cast iron (well-drilling) pipe. At most this amounted to about 700 pounds, but with her engine, which had been installed in 1945, her topsides and waterline had a much better appearance. Her hollow spar and Marconi rig, which eliminated the heavy gaff and telegraph-pole mast, helped her stand up and sail.

163

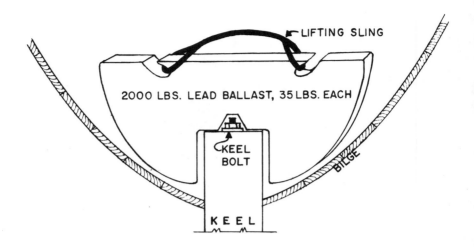

It was not until the early 1950's that I took further action on the ballast problem. Just how does one go about purchasing a ton of lead? Well, the friend of a friend owned a blast furnace used for melting down nonferrous scrap metal. He did not normally deal in lead but he was playing the commodity market one day when the *Wall Street Journal* showed lead to be at an all-time low (35¢ per pound), he placed an order for a ton to be delivered to Bedell's shipyard, Stratford, Connecticut—in my name. In due course, the lead arrived in the form of 27 75-pound pigs. I was on a diet at the time, trying to get my weight below 200 pounds. After manhandling the old iron out of the bilge and overboard to the ground below, and then struggling up the ladder with 27 75-pound pigs and lowering them into the bilge, I weighed 196 pounds. But after the ensuing celebration I bounded right back over 200 again!

It was amazing how little space that lead occupied compared to the much smaller weight of iron. It bothered me to have it stowed loosely under the cabin sole, with the pigs resting directly on the planking, but the difference in the way *Direction* sailed was simply amazing. I now owned a really decent sailboat which could hold her own, even to competing in the Off Soundings races of that year (and coming in last). So, while I never took the boat out of the Nantucket-Long Island Sound circuit, the loose ballast did not worry me too much.

It was another matter, however, when I began making plans to sail to Nova Scotia and Newfoundland. Again, thanks to the Mitchel Refining Company of Portland, Connecticut, I learned of a one-man foundry in Bridgeport that would be willing to recast my lead pigs. So, that winter, when *Direction* was hauled at the Dutch Wharf Boat Yard in Branford, I fashioned a pattern out of wood for the new "pigs". (*See drawing.*) It sat like an inverted "U" on the keelson, with the outer edges faired to the shape of the narrowest parts of the bilge. The pattern was only one inch thick, and I had horns cut into the top to take a battery lifter— for setting and removing the new "pigs" from the bilge.

After five 400-pound trips to the foundry in my car, at intervals of a week or so, I had 60 35-pound shapes of lead that could be conveniently set down on the keelson with no weight touching the planking. I had made a cut-out in the pattern for several pigs that rested over the keel-bolt nuts and washers. It was a neat arrangement, and I was proud of it. Next I cut heavy lengths of 1½-inch oak to fit over the lead and between the floor timbers. On the edges I secured cleats and through the cleats I set heavy lag screws into the floor timbers. I believe this will keep the lead pigs from coming adrift in a knock-down, but am not anxious to give it a test.

ON RUSTY KEEL BOLTS

WHILE BEATING EASTWARD in Long Island Sound at 5:15 A.M. on Sunday, September 29, 1963, in a blow that eventually reached gale force, the beautiful 42-foot, 26-year old schooner *Blackfish* came about off Horton's Point. She just kept on heeling to the other tack until—inside of 30 seconds—her masts and sails were in the water.

Her owner, M. B. Littlefield, was in his bunk fully dressed and about to come on watch. He later told me he felt a jarring wrench, like striking a rock, then heard a crash and tearing noise—which he interpreted as the sound of the keel bolts passing through the cast iron keel as it slipped off its fastenings and dropped to the bottom of Long Island Sound.

One of the crew was in the head at the time and had a grim scramble in the dark through the horizontal cabin which was rapidly filling. In no time *Blackfish* was awash, lying on her side.

The crew stayed with her by standing on the port side tied to lines. Seas, caused by the strong southeast wind and outgoing tide, frequently passed completely over the schooner. By 8:45 A.M. she had drifted to a point about six miles north of the tank farm lying west of Mattituck. The crew decided that under the existing weather conditions there would be no traffic in the area and that the southeast squalls would increase in intensity. The possibility of rescue seemed remote. All five men climbed into a 13-foot Swampscott dory with two rowing thwarts. After rowing two and a half hours they reached the gas buoy which marked the fuel-unloading station, and there they were taken in tow by an outboard boat and towed into Mattituck Inlet. Subsequently, *Blackfish* came ashore at Sound Beach, Greenport, where she eventually broke up.

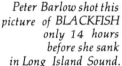

Peter Barlow shot this picture of BLACKFISH only 14 hours before she sank in Long Island Sound.

After writing the above article for the *CCA News* in 1964 I began to worry about *Direction's* keel bolts, as they were 10 years older than those on *Blackfish*. A great many other owners of older boats were no doubt worried, too. I decided to write a follow-up article for the *CCA News,* and planned to use photo examples of keel bolts that had been removed for inspection, but I got little cooperation from any of my friends. In the back of their minds was the fear that any such publicity might hamper a future sale of their boats. Even the architect who designed *Blackfish* was most reluctant to be quoted, so the article never was written.

166

Direction was wintering at Bedell's shipyard in Stratford, Connecticut, at the time. Hauled out near her was the 110-year-old *Stoedebeker*, made famous by Philip Rigg's transatlantic crossing from the Mediterranean several years before. She was in derelict condition, having lost her concrete keel on a ledge, but her keel bolts were exposed and intact. They looked as good as new.

"Why?" I asked Ken Bedell.

"Because they are wrought iron," he answered. "Wrought iron does not rust or corrode as quickly as steel or cast iron." I knew that *Direction*'s keel bolts were made of wrought iron but I was still not satisfied. So Ken drilled two 1½-inch holes, one on each side of the aftermost keel bolt, right at the junction between the wood and the iron keels. Then, with a chisel, he cleared out the space between the holes, revealing a greasy, healthy-looking section of 1½-inch wrought iron bolt. After I inspected it, he filled the cavity with epoxy putty. Ken said that most keel bolts fail right at the junction between the wooden keel and the iron shoe, and I have confirmed that statement several times since then when inspecting keel bolts removed from other boats.

We inspected the bolt farthest aft as, being nearest to the bronze prop and shaft, it would be the most exposed to electrolysis. Presumably, those farther forward would be in better shape. The same principle applies to fastenings, and I have observed this to be dramatically true whenever we have removed a garboard or plank from *Direction*. Boat nails in the same plank are progressively rustier *the farther aft* they are located.

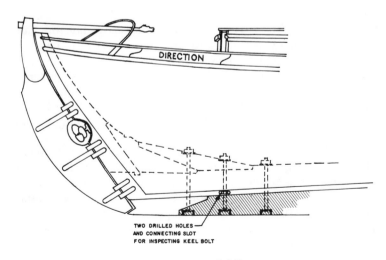

DIRECTION

TWO DRILLED HOLES
AND CONNECTING SLOT
FOR INSPECTING KEEL BOLT

167

Evidence points to *Blackfish* having retained the keel bolts in the boat, with the failure occurring at the bolt heads on the bottom of the iron keel. Possibly they were not real heads, but only peened-over metal such as I have seen on another boat. If such were the case, the reserve of metal to resist corrosion would be only a fraction of what a true head would provide.

A year later Bedell bought a travel lift and we were able to raise *Direction* high enough to get underneath her to inspect the boltheads countersunk in the keel. They all appeared to be in good condition. The nuts and washers on top of the keelson in the bilges looked just fine. In spite of such reassurance one never knows for certain. For this reason I follow the advice of Lit Littlefield, owner of *Blackfish,* "Stow enough inside ballast to keep your boat upright without her keel."

WHEN ROT REARS ITS UGLY HEAD

WOOD IS BIODEGRADABLE. Fiberglass is not. Until the arrival of the plastic boat it was a rare wooden vessel that did not get "recycled" automatically within a century, usually much sooner than that. Witness the efforts and vast expense to keep the *USS Constitution* and the *Charles W. Morgan* afloat beyond their allotted time. Had Queen Isabella provided Christopher Columbus with a caravel of gelcoat, roving, mat, glass cloth and polyester resins, the *Santa Maria* might not have spent a year sitting aground on a reef in the Caribbean while teredos feasted on her hull—and history might have been quite different.

At the rate fiberglass boats are being produced today, the saturation point cannot be far off, and the question is how can we recycle them and avoid unsightly junk yards of boats outclassed by changes or lack of changes in the I.O.R. rule. There is no denying, nevertheless, that the plastic boat has been a blessing to the yachtsman, who at least may eliminate rot from his long list of problems. Only die-hard sentimentalists like me still cling to old wooden boats.

I had not owned *Direction* very long before signs of rot began to appear. She had spent the years of World War II under a canvas cover, both summer and winter, with dampness and sun doing their best to return her to nature. Soon after the war, Walter Pinaud tooks steps to remedy this situation. Much planking—both deck and topsides—was replaced by him. When I bought the boat, he

168

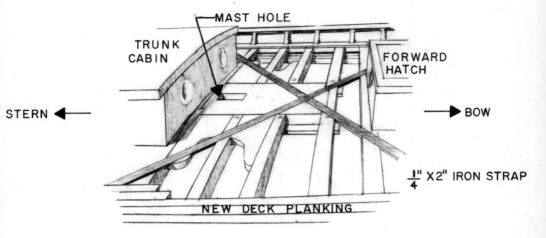

MAST HOLE

TRUNK
CABIN

FORWARD
HATCH

STERN ◀——

——▶ BOW

$\frac{1}{4}$" X 2" IRON STRAP

NEW DECK PLANKING

DIRECTION got new decks in 1959.

was quite frank in describing the work he had done and in admitting that he had not "got it all." But there I was, finally owner of the type boat of which I had dreamed, so I pushed aside thoughts of the problems that might lie ahead. Pinaud predicted that I could get by for 20 years without making any major repairs. In fact, it was 12 years before I was forced to face the inevitable.

Bedell's yard in Stratford, Connecticut, did the job. They removed *Direction's* decks and much of her covering board. This allowed a good look at her beams and partners. Fortunately, Bedell had done no major rebuilding in several years and the oak in his lumber shed had had time to become well seasoned.

When *Direction* was all put back together again she had new Philippine mahogany decks, new oak mast partners, several new lodging knees and hanging knees, and a few 4" x 4" oak deck beams— including a new main beam at the forward end of the trunk cabin. When the bill for the job came, I discovered that I had purchased *Direction* all over again—one and one-half times, to be exact. But I still had my dream boat. Fortunately, my affluence had been upgraded slightly during those 12 years so I was not hurt too badly.

169

Seven years later, this time in Jack Jacques' Dutch Wharf Boat Yard, in Branford, Connecticut, I had to face and eliminate rot once again. That came as no surprise. I had merely been postponing the *real* day of reckoning, and might have prolonged it further if I had not been planning to sail *Direction* back to Nova Scotia. This time, we installed 23 sister frames alongside some questionable ones. To do this, we had to remove the garboards and some perfectly good planking, just to inspect what was underneath. When it came time to put the boat back together again, we fastened with galvanized carriage bolts.

Sections of the deadwood were also removed and some bad parts of the keel were replaced. We drilled deep into the heartwood of the keel (which we would have had to destroy the boat to remove) and inserted copper tubing which led to a funnel into which we poured Calignum over a period of more than a week. The hope was that the Calignum would drain into any inaccessible bad parts of the keel and, after being absorbed, would harden to the consistency of rock.

Jack Jacques runs a high-morale type of boatyard. His men work there because they like him and they love boats, particularly old wooden boats. Jack likes old wooden boats, too, particularly rotten ones with crazy owners like me. He will not lead you down the garden path, however, and if your boat is beyond hope, he will tell you so. When some of *Direction's* planking was removed there was great hilarity among his men as they discovered that the Greenlanders, who had repaired *Direction* after her wreck, had inserted shingles here and there to help fair the planking to the frames—she had been so pounded out of shape during her shipwreck. In fact, we had run into the same problem at Bedell's yard seven years earlier. To get the hog out of her starboard deck over the place where she had hit the rocks, Bedell had had to shave down the deck beam and thin down the decking.

Pride in their craft and skills is such among the men at Dutch Wharf Boat Yard that the shingles did not go back, and somehow or other, by a shipyard magic known only to them, the planking was properly faired to her timbers. When the bill arrived, I discovered that once more I had purchased *Direction all over again,* not merely one and a half times her *original* purchase price, but one and a half times the *aggregate* investment! I still had my dream boat, however, and felt I could sail the northern edge of Georges Bank the following summer with confidence that she would take us on to the Bras d'Or Lakes in comfort and safety.

170

In fact, despite all these bouts with rot, I have never been kept busy at the bilge pump in *Direction*. I pump her out every other week but could go much longer without doing so, and this has been the case ever since I bought her. I have never seen another wooden boat as tight as she has been through the years. Nor have I ever cruised on any other boat in which you never hear any creaking as sailing strains shift back and forth in the hull. It is as if she were cast from one solid piece. I attribute this to her overrugged construction. She has two lengths of 2" x ¼" iron strapping laid diagonally on the deck beams to form an X at her partners, each one connected to her shelf clamps, and let into the tops of her deck beams. Having a forward cabin trunk as well as a main one, the mast passes through the deck between them, imposing its strains there, not on the coach roof. Those full-width deck beams, as well as those in her bridge deck, provide the strength that is missing in many later designs. She has two laminated bilge stringers running the entire length of each bilge. No matter what the stresses, she simply does not "work," and though we may hear galley pans rattling in a seaway, we never hear any creaking from the hull.

I don't for a moment consider that I am through coping with rot. Every year Ralph Pinaud and I go over *Direction* carefully, tapping and listening for the dull thud of bad wood. So far, her planking responds with a healthy resonating ring. Jack Jacques at the Dutch Wharf Boat Yard did a pretty thorough job, and the cool climate on Cape Breton Island, where she has been based for the past 10 years, should slow down the process. Boats in northern latitudes always live longer than those in more temperate climates.

So if you are hankering for a classic boat, you should think twice before doing as I have done. Unless you are prepared to buy your bargain wooden boat over again every few years, you'd better stick to fiberglass.

Photo by Peter Barlow.

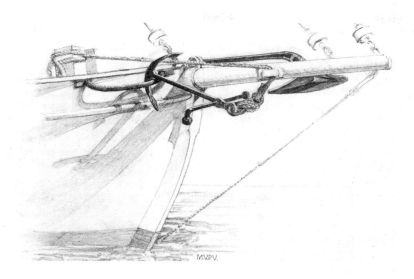

GROUND TACKLE & THE ART
OF ANCHORING

Because I grew up with the old make-and-break, one-lung engines, which would stop dead if a fleck of carbon got on the spark points, I learned early the importance of being able to drop anchor on short notice. Those engines would always start up again, but sometimes you needed either a good anchor or some drifting time and room to save your boat. Also, *Direction's* shipwreck in Greenland served to fortify my instincts along this line, which were that an anchor lying under the floorboards in the bilge is as good as no anchor at all. Rockwell Kent was still struggling to get the heavy anchor up on deck when *Direction* struck the rocks in Karajak Fjord.

It is also important that your anchor take hold promptly and not require so-called "setting room." This is why *Direction* has a kedge anchor made up and slung from her bowsprit with the flukes hung over a curved bronze pipe that is fastened to her starboard bow and designed for just that purpose *(see sketch).* This is also why I would not want a boat without a bowsprit. If your anchor has to be made up every time you use it, or if it digs the paint off your topsides every time you take it up, you tend not to use it.

173

In this age of advertising, the good old kedge anchor has no one to sing its praises. It is not patented so no one has a motive to tout it. The patent-anchor people quite naturally promote their own product, and would like to brainwash the novice sailor into believing it is the only possible one to use. One major manufacturer of lightweight anchors has even printed a graphic history of the anchor in which the kedge is represented as being a step in anchor evolution leading right up to his own product. This is certainly misleading. I carry two patent anchors on my boat, and I find no fault with them and consider them a definite breakthrough in anchor development, *but no single anchor is the answer to all situations.* If I did have but one choice, I would select a heavy kedge, much as I like the Danforth and admire the ingenuity of the plow or C.Q.R.

There is just no substitute for weight, the Messrs. Danforth, *et al,* to the contrary notwithstanding. I don't say this for the benefit of the marina habitué, to whom it is an adventure to anchor out overnight, or the dedicated ocean racer, who watches every pound of weight on his foredeck. I am speaking to the practical cruising man.

I once sailed into Bay Finn of North Channel fame on Lake Huron. We were in Larry Perkins' Chicago-based Alden schooner, *Allegro.* We rounded up under mainsail, dropped her 90-pound kedge, and rowed a stern line ashore to a tree. There was no horsing around. Had that anchor dragged, we might have had to start up the motor (Heaven forbid). But Larry was certain of himself, and we were as snug as we could be. Later, as we sat in the cockpit, relaxing over drinks, one of those chrome-plated top-heavy cruisers from Toronto arrived. We watched as the owner tossed over a 20-pound Danforth and, for the next half hour, proceeded to rake up all the seaweed in the harbor. That anchor never got to within 10 feet of the bottom. Eventually they gave up and left, most likely spending the night in a marina about four miles distant. We were left alone, so promptly drank a toast to Mr. Danforth, and a second one to the marina that attracts so many noisy power cruisers, leaving us alone to savor the peace of that charming harbour.

Now Larry Perkins does not scorn the Danforth anchor. In her inventory, *Allegro* carries a five-pounder, among others. This is used as a lunch hook and under proper conditons holds that 43-foot schooner adequately. On the power cruiser, the 20-pound Danforth was apparently her sole bit of ground tackle.

We were aboard Dave Bacon's ketch, *Sandpiper*, one time in the Saint John River, New Brunswick, and tossed his 20-pound Danforth onto an exposed mudbank left by a dredge. As we backed against it, it dragged a few inches, reared up and plunged its flukes straight down to disappear completely. It held like a ton of bricks and gave visual demonstration of how these anchors behave when given the right kind of bottom and scope. Here was a situation in which the Danforth most definitely had it all over the kedge.

On board *Direction*, as mentioned above, I carry a 42-pound kedge permanently made up on the starboard side of the bowsprit, with one fluke hooked into a bronze loop. Where the shank joins the flukes I have secured a six-foot line with an eye splice and large knot on the opposite end. This line goes to the bottom with the anchor. When we haul up the anchor and it is dangling from the bowsprit, I can reach down with a boat hook and catch the knot or the loop, and bring it up within reach. From there I haul up the line, lifting only *half* the weight of the anchor, and easily drop one fluke over the bronze loop. Anchoring by this system is no effort at all.

On the port side of the bowsprit, I carry a 35-pound plow anchor with 20 feet of chain which is shackled and spliced into a nylon anchor rode. This anchor, too, is easy to handle. It fits snugly into a roller chock large enough to pass the splice, thimble and shackle of the chain. The ⅝-inch nylon rode is short—60 feet to be exact—so I can easily buoy the whole works and slip it overboard should the need arise. The kedge has 250 feet of ⅝-inch rode. Both rodes are stowed on deck. Ninety percent of the time, we use the kedge. It is by far the easiest to handle and the most certain to dig in quickly, and hold.

175

On deck, also on the port side, I carry an 85-pound yachtsman's-type kedge anchor with the stock folded alongside the shank. It is secured by lanyards to deck rings and pads. There is a 200-foot length of one-inch nylon anchor rode in the port chain locker below decks, with the end fastened to a hook on the hawse-pipe cap so as to be easily accessible from deck. This is our storm anchor.

Because of *Direction's* heavy construction, deep forefoot and fullness forward, she can easily carry this weight, whereas the light-displacement cruiser would be overburdened.

On the starboard side I carry a 65-pound C.Q.R. anchor, also on pads, but shackled to 15 feet of ⅜-inch chain, which in turn is shackled to a 30-foot length of one-inch nylon, ending in a large eye splice. In the starboard chain locker I keep 300 feet of ⅞-inch nylon rode. This C.Q.R. being all made up can serve as a temporary mooring, and I keep a float below decks to attach to the splice should I wish to use it that way. Being the most nonfouling of all, except possibly a mushroom anchor, I can set the C.Q.R. in any harbor where I plan to stay for a while and want my own private mooring. When I want to use it as a storm anchor, I merely bend the end of the 300 feet of nylon to the eye splice and pay out scope. The plow anchor is the American version of the original C.Q.R., the principle difference between them being that the C.Q.R. has a lead-weighted point whereas the plow does not. This leaded point is very important to insure digging into a hard bottom, but is anathema to the naval architect trying to reduce weight up forward on racing craft.

176

I am certain that some readers will snort at all this overkill, but in *Direction* I have the luxury of both deck space and capacity for weight, and it is my firm belief that no anchor ever carried is heavy enough for the ultimate situation. So why not have *all* the insurance you can afford?

Chafing gear is important if you have to ride out a blow at anchor where there is any motion. I keep lengths of rubber hose right on my two storm anchor rodes down in the chain locker. If one is needed I can slip it along the rode up close to the bollards, then let out scope until the chafing gear is in the correct position.

I am not recommending that the reader do as I do regarding anchors. There are plenty of good reasons for keeping only light gear on deck. But you never know when you may lose an anchor, or have to "slip" your anchor to avoid a drifting boat, or you may simply want them on deck permanently for convenience. It is a great comfort to know that you have spare anchors in reserve, especially a really heavy one that you might not be able even to recover once it is used; but, if it saves your boat from going ashore, so what? I want at least one quick-setting anchor, available *at once*. I also want reserve anchoring capabilities both in heft and quantity. Fortunately *Direction* can carry all this equipment without being overburdened.

Another point the patent-anchor people make is that it is far easier to raise a light anchor than a heavy one. That is true, but again, *Direction* is not bothered by our powerful, hand-operated windlass. Most modern yacht owners are reluctant to fit one, again because of the weight. What a pity!

DIRECTION in the Mystic River. Photo by Merrill Lindsay.

ON ELECTRICITY

BECAUSE WE had never enjoyed the luxury of electricity aboard a boat until we owned *Direction*, it never had seemed important. Nor had *Direction* ever had it until just before we purchased her. She had a generating set to charge her 12-volt lighting system which had been in operation for only one season when we got her.

We did not trust it, however, and about the only change that we requested of Mr. Pinaud after moving aboard was the substitution of combination kerosene and electric running lights for the electric lights he had installed. In the 30 now years of owning her we have had to fall back on the kerosene running lights exactly once. However, we have kept the combination lights so that we can be independent of electricity when at sea. I no longer keep the lamps filled with kerosene, but at least they can be filled and lit in fairly short order should the need arise.

What we did like about the arrangement was that starting the engine was done with a system completely separate from the one generating the lights. In fact, it was a six-volt system running off a generator connected by belt to the fly-wheel. This required running the one-cylinder generating plant occasionally to make electricity, which was a bother in a quiet anchorage at night and a nuisance under way. It was a comfort, however, to know that no matter how late we or our guests read in bed, the engine would start the next morning.

In 1965 we installed a Westerbeke 4-107 diesel engine which develops 37 hp, and removed the separate generating plant. (This also meant that we no longer had to carry gasoline aboard.) For the lights we had an alternator, and for starting the engine we had a generator, both run by power take-off sheaves on the Westerbeke. The electrical systems were totally indpendent, although I have jumper cables aboard to connect the two systems— just in case.

I do not approve of the popular system of having a rotary switch that can be turned to "Battery No. 1," "Battery No. 2," "Both" or "Off," for the simple reason that a guest can make a mistake, turn the switch while the motor is running and burn out the alternator. There also is the temptation to use the starting batteries for lights once the lighting batteries get low. I want my starting batteries to be 100 percent reliable and to be used for nothing else. Also, I feel more secure having them charged by a generator and not the much more efficient but less reliable alternator.

On our old engine, the starting solenoid was not totally enclosed, and if for some reason it failed (as is bound to happen eventually) you could reach under it and push the solenoid up to actuate the self-starter. This is not true of any of the modern solenoids that I have seen. For this reason I have had made up a short jumper wire that will contact the posts on each side of the solenoid so I can get the motor started and keep on starting it till I can get somewhere to purchase a new solenoid. This happened to us some years ago on Stafford Johnson's *Windrose,* a twin-screw powerboat with GM 4-53's. When we reached Thunderbolt,Georgia, there was another boat there with the same trouble. It was unable to move, however, as the owner had not thought of jumping the solenoid. A GM mechanic serviced both boats and showed us the paper-thin sheet of copper used for the contacts which had failed in our solenoids.

Before we departed for Nova Scotia in 1966, Jack Jacques at the Dutch Wharf marina had an electronics expert come aboard *Direction* with an ohm meter to check out the electric potentials, and bond the stove, engine and other metal parts to the keel, to give us as much protection from electrolysis as possible. I accept this electrical tinkering on faith; it is all Mumbo Jumbo to me.

179

ON STOVES

MY INTRODUCTION TO the kerosene-burning Primus galley stove occurred in 1931 when I hired a wherry from Salter's Boat Livery in Oxford, England, and rowed 150 miles down the Thames River to London. I camped each night along the way for more than a week, stopping at such historic places as Runnemede, Windsor, and Henley, and a myriad less distinguished but no less charming spots. My previous experience had been with the alcohol-burning stove I had aboard my catboat, *Nancy Lee.* I had been told that alcohol was clean, did not have a disagreeable smell and could be extinguished by water if you had a stove fire. All true! But alcohol gives much less heat, is much more expensive, is hard to find in remote places, and *has* caused uncontrollable fires that water has failed to extinguish.

That 17-foot camping rowboat was a revelation to me, equipped with a tent that fitted over its entire length, seats that could be removed for unrolling a mattress and sleeping bag, 10-foot spoon-blade cedar oars, and the marvelous, kerosene-burning Primus stove. Since that experience I have cruised on boats equipped with bottled gas or alcohol and have witnessed the care and apprehension with which propane must be handled, and the dangerous galley fires that all too frequently flare up with alcohol, and I have always had a kerosene-burning Primus stove aboard my own boats.

180

For the past 45 years, *Direction* has had either a Shipmate or a Lunenburg stove, each of which burned coal, wood, or charcoal briquettes. When we bought her, we added a two-burner Primus stove which sits atop the Shipmate for hot-weather cooking. As most readers know the Primus is a pressure-type stove with a central tank equipped with an air pump. The liquid kerosene is vaporized initially by priming a "heat generator" with an alcohol flame, and, when the kerosene is burning, is vaporized by its own generated heat. So what actually burns is the gas of vaporized kerosene. In nearly 45 years experience with it, I have never witnessed a kerosene galley fire. True, a bright yellow flame will flare up if you ignite the kerosene before it has become properly vaporized, but this only happens when you are at the controls and can quickly shut off the burner—at which point the flame subsides promptly.

In chilly weather, our Primus is stored on a shelf in the forward cabin and we enjoy the cozy warmth produced by our Lunenburg coal stove. That is, we did until 1973, when we finally went "modern" and bought a pot-type oil stove. But let me tell you about our beloved Lunenburg first. Our Lunenburg No. 12 Fisherman stove is the same size as the standard U. S. Shipmate stove familiar to so many yachtsmen. It is produced by the Lunenburg Foundry of Lunenburg, Nova Scotia. My wife and I spent two days in February 1973 visiting the foundry and watching the workers assemble these stoves, some of smaller sizes and several of much larger sizes. In our 30 years with *Direction* we have had three of these stoves. They were so inexpensive that when they rusted out we simply replaced them. Freight and duty from Nova Scotia added to the price, but it still was only a fraction of the cost of a Shipmate. One time I tried replacing the rusted-out top of the stove and the shipyard bill for installing it came to twice what a new stove would have cost, so I did not indulge in that doubtful economy again!

What joy it is to wake up on a cold morning, light a fire of crackling chips of teak and mahogany (gleaned from the floor underneath Pinaud's band saw), pour on a little hard coal and climb back into your bunk! The singing of the kettle soon informs you that it is time to rise again, strip naked in front of the radiant heat of the black iron stove, take a sponge bath, and dress for the day.

Those cold, damp watches in the icy fog of Georges Bank or off the coast of Newfoundland become delights when you can look down the hatch at a glowing coal fire with a pot of coffee simmering away, waiting for you to come off watch! Even the sound of the coal shovel as the stove is stoked has nostalgic associations of warmth and cozy comfort.

Our coal bunker was filled through a deck plate, and occupied an entire frame bay beneath the stove. A trap door opened under the stove, just the width of the coal shovel, so it was easy, relatively clean and convenient to add fuel. We could carry 150 pounds of coal, which would last us through the summer when the stove was lit only on cold or damp days. This was not enough capacity for a July-August cruise in Newfoundland, however, and we had trouble finding coal along that coast. In recent years, while living aboard through October at Cape Breton Island, we found we were consuming 500 pounds per month, but since we were on our home mooring it was a simple matter to keep a reserve ashore.

Then Pinaud's yard lost its source of supply of hard coal. Dr. Paul B. Sheldon had been in the habit of stowing 500 pounds of hard coal (imported from Scotland) aboard his 36-foot *Seacrest* for his trips down the Labrador, but even this was not enough to get him through a full summer's cruising. When Pinaud could no longer provide the hard coal, Paul switched to the locally mined soft coal, and we began thinking about a shift to oil. With a stove burning "stove oil" we would have no trouble obtaining fuel on the south coast of Newfoundland. Most of the homes in those villages are heated with stove oil, using the same kind of burners as the one we might install.

That was the reason for our tip to Lunenburg in February 1973. We watched in the Lunenburg Foundry as pot-type oil burners were being installed in our Fisherman No. 12 model, as well as several other models. They all required blowers, which in turn required electricity and, presumably, made a noise when running. With our old generating set removed, we could not afford the electricity needed for the long October nights at anchor in the Washabuckt River. What to do?

A pot-type burner vaporizes fuel into a gas by having a heavy metal combustion chamber perforated with holes to let in air. Fuel passes through what they call a "carburetor," which actually is a very delicate metering valve. The heat of the metal pot vaporizes the surface of the fuel which ignites as air passes through the perforations. It produces a silent, hot flame. Proper draft is essential to avoid incomplete combustion, which would cause accumulation of carbon and soot. This was why the Lunenburg Foundry people insisted upon a blower; they were just too honest

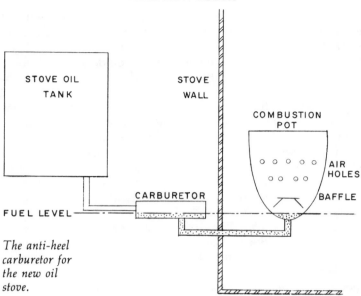

STOVE OIL
TANK

STOVE
WALL

COMBUSTION
POT

AIR
HOLES

CARBURETOR

BAFFLE

FUEL LEVEL

*The anti-heel
carburetor for
the new oil
stove.*

and conscientious to let me buy a stove without one. So, for the
moment, we gave up the idea.

I was aware that in Sackville, New Brunswick, the Enterprise
Stove Company was manufacturing a Fawcett Columbia brand of
stove, engineered specially for boats. The question was: Would
they sell me a stove without a blower when in fact it really needed
one? In the spring of 1973 when we arrived at Pinaud's yard to
commission *Direction*, Ralph had already installed a Columbia
oil stove on a local Cape Island lobster boat. My wife and I inspected it and were greatly impressed. Ralph Pinaud was so certain of the stoves that he had ordered three. One of them was
meant for *Direction*, but I did not suspect his intention at the time.
Ralph, with his knowledge of my psychology, just kept quiet,
believing that eventually I would tell him to install it on *Direction*.

On our way to Connecticut for a brief visit home in August, we
visited the Enterprise Company just to take a look. As luck would
have it, that day they had a whole battery of "our" type of stove
on line for testing. Whereas the Lunenburg stoves were conver-
sions, these were designed from scratch to burn oil and to achieve
proper draft *without* a blower. After everything had been explained and demonstrated to us, we continued on our way
toward Connecticut with our misgivings diminished considerably.

I made my decision while we were at home and phoned Ralph to go ahead and install the stove, specifying that the "carburetor" be shifted so as to be on axis with the pot inlet *and* the heel of the boat under sail. This was so that it would not be higher on one tack than on the other, because the flow of fuel was entirely by gravity.

We returned to Baddeck to find our new and shiny stove installed. It was supplied by an 11-gallon stainless steel fuel tank underneath the bridge deck, where it replaced an old unused water tank. The stove oil was piped from this tank to a "carburetor" underneath the sink, thence to the stove which had been surrounded with asbestos-stainless steel lining. It did not have the character and romance of our old Lunenburg, but it did look pretty good!

We consume one 55-gallon drum of stove oil in six weeks, from mid-September to the end of October. We keep the stove going on a low flame all night. The temperature may drop to 25° Fahrenheit outdoors during darkness, yet we wake up to a 68° temperature in the main cabin. The stove is silent, clean and, as far as I can make out, perfectly safe.

We tried to create down-drafts to see if we could blow the stove out or make it smoke. With one person standing to leeward of the smoke head in a heavy blow, we could produce a down-draft and smoking, but the baffle plate over the flame prevented the flame from blowing out. We had one 30-35 knot wind in which we sailed close-hauled under a deep-reefed main and forestaysail, in smooth, sheltered water. There was no adverse effect on the stove on either tack. The only time the stove has blown out was one time when our cockpit tent was set over the main hatch in a rainstorm, creating a back-draft down the stove pipe. This is a danger that must be watched for when relighting the stove. With the flame out and the hot pot continuing to vaporize the fuel, there could be a dangerous explosion if one were to touch a match to it. So the proper procedure, if the flame goes out, is to let the stove cool, bail out any surplus oil and relight the stove from scratch. The lighting procedure is simply to let in some oil with the setting at "START" on the carburetor, and drop some burning Kleenex into the stove. Give the pot time to heat up, then turn the dial to the desired setting. We have exchanged the romance of wood smoke for the practicality of effortless oil comfort. I am not certain as yet which I cherish the most.

*MALAY and DIRECTION meet by
chance in Francois. MALAY with
her inflatable on her coach roof,
and DIRECTION with her rigid
Grumman dinghy on the foredeck.*

ON DINGHYS, THEIR USE AND STOWAGE

I FEEL STRONGLY that, if possible, a cruising boat should
carry a rigid dinghy. If your boat is too small to do so, then you
ought not go anywhere you can't tow a dinghy. For myself, I like
a dinghy burdensome enough to carry a heavy anchor out to windward. To do this, you must be able to row the dinghy effectively
through a chop and against the wind without depending on an
outboard motor. I want a dinghy in which my wife can go ashore
in city clothes and high heels without getting wet. I want a dinghy
that will not take off like a kite when hit by a squall. I want a
dingy that. will not be punctured by coral or a rough stony beach.
I want a dinghy that is not only easy to row, but a pleasure to
row, so that if I chose to anchor well out, it is fun to row ashore.
These are personal prejudices, acquired from first-hand experiences with both inflatable and rigid dinghies. I am not telling
anyone what to do; I am only explaining what I do, and why.

185

When our daughter was growing up, I felt the need for two dinghies. We had a Dyer Midget, a sailing model 7'6" long. It was built of mahogany plywood. Later, I purchased one of Bill Dyer's earliest fiberglass nine-foot rowing dinghies. The seats are held in place by bronze brackets that are attached to the seats and to the gunwales with four round-head screws. I cut slots in the screwholes in the gunwale end of the bronze brackets *(see sketch)* and kept the screws backed out a turn. It was then easy to lift the center and front seats right out of the nine-footer and store the smaller sailing dinghy inside it. This gave me a "rescue" boat aboard, when my young daughter was learning to sail solo. I stored the two dinghies nested and upside down on the forward deck, thus using only the space of one. I used this setup until my daughter grew up and went off to college.

I have never liked the oars that come with dinghies. They are always too short and rarely a pleasure to row. They are short, I suspect, so as to stow easily inside the boat. It seems to me that manufacturers have lost sight of the basic principles of rowing, or else they do not care because they cater to an ignorant public. Regardless of the kind of boat you are rowing, 6'6" oars are the minimum for efficient propulsion and 7' to 7'6" are much better. With shorter oars, you lose your leverage and get a windmill effect, expending too much energy for the distance you get out of a stroke.

I do not care for the oarlocks that come with dinghies, either. Any time-and-motion study man could tell you they are as inefficient as short oars. The standard U-shaped oarlock, provided with new boats, is fastened by a chain to the gunwales to prevent its loss overboard. It must be set in the socket and removed in a separate operation from shipping the oars. This requires an extra action by the hands which are still holding the oars. If you wish to shift rowing stations, you must first set the oars down, then, with both hands, work the toggle on the chain to remove one oarlock from the socket, move it, set it in the new socket, then repeat the process with the other oarlock.

But if you have a ring-type oarlock, permanently fastened to the oar, moving oarlocks and shipping oars is accomplished instantly in one sweeping motion with both hands. I have leathers on my oars, with collars that keep the round oarlocks from slipping off the ends. With these I can let go of my oars while they are still shipped, or even while one is unshipped as I go alongside *Direction*, to hand up baggage or help a guest. The oarlocks

186

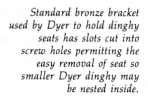

Standard bronze bracket used by Dyer to hold dinghy seats has slots cut into screw holes permitting the easy removal of seat so smaller Dyer dinghy may be nested inside.

Ring-type oarlocks held in place with leather collars make shipping oars a much faster and safer operation.

are *always* with the oars, where you want them. There is no chance of leaving them in the sockets to gouge your topsides. The only fault to be found with this setup is that a novice, digging too deeply with the oars, can split the gunwales of the boat. This has happened to me just once.

In my flotilla of small craft I also have a Grumman aluminum rowing dinghy, and a Grumman canoe. The dinghy carries 7′6″ spoon-blade cedar oars with the same ring-type oarlocks and leathers as my Dyer dinghy oars. The oars just barely stow inside the Grumman dinghy and are a bit too long for a novice to row comfortably, but they are so efficient that I never feel the need for an outboard motor. This dinghy weighs only 85 pounds, which is the main reason I keep it with *Direction* in Nova Scotia. The

187

Dyer nine-foot dinghy weighs 110 pounds. The Grumman dinghy will capsize if someone inadvertently sits on the front seat when no one else is in the boat to act as a counterbalance, whereas the Dyer has much more stability. Twice I have had fully dressed guests in city clothes get a dunking in the Grumman dinghy. However, when properly loaded and handled, both boats are tops for towing, rowing and seaworthiness.

The Grumman canoe is made of light-gauge aluminum; it is 13 feet long and weighs 41 pounds. In the 15 years that I have owned it, it has been a great joy. Were it not for the fact that I keep it on board *Direction* I would have had a 17-footer for greater stability and safety, but this 13-footer fits on deck when we are cruising Long Island Sound or exploring the Bras d'Or Lakes, with the Grumman dinghy in tow. I do not take the canoe to sea as I need the deck space for the dinghy which is our lifeboat and workhorse, whereas the canoe is a luxury. The canoe also fits as easily both on my wife's small station wagon, as on my larger station wagon. It has become so much a part of our life that it commutes back and forth with us on every trip between Connecticut and Cape Breton Island.

Along the route we know of motels and cottages where we spend the night, and we frequently enjoy an evening paddle on a quiet Maine lake after a long day's drive. We have carried the canoe as far as Charlevoix, Michigan, where we put it on the deck of Larry Perkins' Alden schooner, *Allegro*, for intimate exploration of the North Channel and Georgian Bay. Similarly, we have had it in the Saint John River of New Brunswick aboard Dave Bacon's *Sandpiper*. It has a padded carrying yoke that I keep permanently attached to the center thwart and I can carry it on my soulders with no effort. There is just no end to the pleasures to be had with a canoe that can be taken wherever you go.

ON TILLERS AND STEERING

IT NEVER occurred to me to check a tiller for rot until *Direction's* came off in my hands one day as we were running before a fresh southwesterly off Cuttyhunk. We had been on the starboard tack, so when we rounded up with the mainsail luffing, we were headed right for the Sow and Pigs reef off the westerly tip of the island. There was sufficient sea room if I worked fast enough.

*Seth Persson of Saybrook, Connecticut,
carved a new tiller for DIRECTION.*

I reversed the tiller and, using the handle end as a ramrod, forced out the rotten end remaining in the rudder head. This Colin Archer-type outboard rudder is simplicity to perfection. A heavy oak "cheek" is fastened to each side of the rudder head with many bolts. These cheeks extend above the rudder and are connected with a cap on top. The tiller is morticed into the cavity thus created to form (if the wood is only good) an almost foolproof arrangement. With an axe, I shaved down what was left of the thick part of the tiller until I could insert it into the rudder head aperture, and we were on our way again with a tiller eight inches shorter than before.

That incident gave me a good excuse to ask Seth Persson of Saybrook, Connecticut, where we left *Direction* each winter, if he would carve a new tiller for us like one his father had carved many years before. Seth kept a photograph of his father's tiller in his office. The original had the head of a Norse gargoyle carved on the handle, with fierce teeth, glowering eyes and protruding tongue.

189

I drove to the yard one day that fall after the boat had been laid up, and Seth showed me a clay half-model of what he proposed to do. I was delighted and gave him the go-ahead. All that winter, as a sort of recreational project in the evenings, Seth whittled away on a piece of 4" x 6" oak, seven feet long. The accompanying sketch shows the results. It was Seth's first attempt at such an ambitious carving. During that same winter in Saybrook, he was building the Fenwick Williams-designed catboat, *Tabby*, for the late John Killam Murphy, and later Seth was commissioned by Carleton Mitchell to build the famous *Finisterre*.

There are times when a weather helm will put a lot of strain on the tiller, and I ease the helmsman's job by using a tiller line that can also be adjusted to make *Direction* steer herself for considerable periods of time. I slip the eye splice on the end of this tiller line over the tiller, lead it around to a horizontal pin in the bulwarks stanchion and then back, where I wind it around the tiller at least 12 times, ending in a clove hitch. I call this my "micrometer adjustable automatic pilot." I usually wet the end of the line that winds around the tiller. This provides enough friction so that the line will not unwind, and for any minor steering adjustment you simply grab the entire coil and clove hitch and twist it, thus making a "very fine" change in the position of the tiller.

ON GALLOWS FRAMES

WHEN WE first acquired *Direction*, she was equipped with her original scissors-type boom crutch to hold up an extremely heavy boom. Even in a quiet harbor it was a struggle to set up the crutch (with the boom in it) for furling the mainsail. This was one of several features that ruled out *Direction* as a singlehander in those early years. It was positively dangerous to reef or try to lower the mainsail at sea. A gallows frame presented a problem because *Direction* is double ended, so I had the Bedell yard make me the horizontal part of a gallows frame out of oak, with three notches in it, and a hinged central member that lifted the boom an extra eight inches once the sail was furled. I purchased a pipe-bending tool and some 1¼-inch heavy bronze pipe. I bent the pipe to fit the contours of the stern. Then Bedell, after determining the proper shape, brazed the pipe to bronze plates which he bolted to the bulwarks, and then bolted the upper ends to the oak crosspiece.

Now, when I am alone on the boat and entering a harbor to anchor, I can let the boat luff up by herself while I go forward, release the main halyard and drop the boom into the center notch. The outside notches are handy in case I miss, or for tying in a reef while under way. The gallows frame also serves as a handhold for anyone standing in the stern.

On a double-ender, a gallows frame will not work in conjunction with roller-reefing gear on the main boom, as the main sheet could not lead to a traveler and still clear the frame. This applies only to a double-ended boat.

I set up the topping lift just loose enough to allow the boom to rest in any of the three lower notches across the gallows frame. Then, when the boom is lifted eight inches by the extra hinged notch, or when under sail, a piece of shock cord keeps the topping lift taut and it does not slap against the roach of the sail. I plan to replace the present wire topping lift with plastic-coated lifeline wire, to reduce further the possibility of sail chafe. Today, looking back, it seems unthinkable to me that I ever tolerated that dangerous, awkward scissors-type boom crutch.

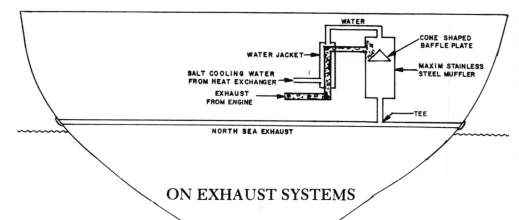

WATER
CONE SHAPED BAFFLE PLATE
WATER JACKET→
MAXIM STAINLESS STEEL MUFFLER
SALT COOLING WATER FROM HEAT EXCHANGER→
EXHAUST FROM ENGINE→
TEE
NORTH SEA EXHAUST

ON EXHAUST SYSTEMS

WHEN *Direction* had her first (gasoline) engine installed in 1945, after going 16 years without one, Walter Pinaud did such a good job that I have never wanted to change the basic arrangement in any way, even when I replaced it with the Westerbeke diesel. So it has come as a shock to me since then to see so many modern yachts whose builders have either ignored or been ignorant of the basic good sense that was second nature to Mr. Pinaud.

On a modern fiberglass boat, I have stepped out of my bunk into water six inches deep over the cabin sole, due to the exhaust line being *below* the waterline with corrosion eating a hole in it and thus nearly sinking the boat. I have been told of exhaust systems on sailboats that have a valve that must be shut when under way so that the water will not back up into the engine. I hear noisy installations chugging past my Branford home disturbing the peace of a Sunday afternoon and wonder how the crew can stand it. None of this is necessary.

The exhaust for the engines I have had in *Direction* has led to a muffler under the bridge deck, well above the water line, then down to a "T," which has an exhaust pipe going out both the port and starboard sides. This is sometimes called a "North Sea Exhaust." The entire system is visible and accessible, with no long pipe running out to the stern to submerge in a following sea or remain hidden and difficult to inspect. My present muffler is a stainless steel Maxim that sprays cooling water over a baffle, condensing the exhaust gasses so that I only need a 1¼-inch pipe to lead out either side of the boat.

192

When I installed the Westerbeke 4-107 in 1965 I feared it might be noisy so I left room for a second in-line muffler just in case. But with the condensing type of muffler, the engine is as quiet as the two previous gasoline engines. Rarely am I aware of diesel fumes from the exhaust, since they go out the sides of the boat; they are never worse than with a stern exhaust. This exhaust system has the added advantage that there is always one exhaust pipe above water when the boat heels.

ON RADIOS AND ELECTRONIC GEAR

IN THE EARLY 1920's, I first cruised with a portable radio, or "wireless receiver" as they were called then. That was aboard my brother's Crosby catboat, on which I crewed before owning a boat of my own. The cost of the radio seemed astronomical to us, so we only used it on one sail off Execution Lighthouse. It consisted of a box the size of a small suitcase, laden with a heavy ballast of "A" batteries and "B" batteries, and God only knows what else. The loop antenna, which doubled as the cover, was removable and had to be inserted by one corner into the top. Then the set was turned on. After a prolonged warm-up period, we could hear—amidst much crackling—the voice of an announcer extolling L. Bamburger and Company in Newark, New Jersey, and using the call letters WOR.

We were thrilled by this experience but looked upon it as a novelty with little practical value. There was no such thing as a weather broadcast, so far as we knew, at least nothing oriented to the yachtsman, nor did it ever occur to us to expect such a service. It was 20 years later, during World War II, that a portable radio became a fixture aboard my own boat. It still had tubes that had to be warmed up, and the batteries weighed like bricks. But by then there were regular weather broadcasts and news reports that were quite useful. The notion of owning a radiotelephone had not even occurred to me. Such a thing was fine on large expensive yachts, but with the hand-cranked, one-cylinder, 8-hp Universal Fisherman engine I then had, it was out of the question even to think about.

When I purchased *Direction* in 1946 I considered buying an RDF, but they seemed prohibitively expensive, took up too much space, and were practically unobtainable in that first year after World War II. So, we came down the coast of Nova Scotia and across to Cape Cod, depending upon our Negus taffrail log, chronometer watch, vernier sextant, deep-sea lead and compass. Our only electronic aid was the time tick from WOR which we received on our vacuum-tube portable radio, borrowed from my catboat which we had not yet sold.

So you see, our approach to electronic aids was totally different from that of today's boat owners, most of whom wouldn't think of leaving port without being able to call the Coast Guard if something went wrong. Not that I belittle that attitude. It's only that, since I grew up before it was possible to own a radiotelephone, I had never felt the urgency to do so. Today I feel differently and of this moment I have made application for an operator's and station license, and when I get them I shall invest in a VHF set—mostly in deference to the reality that my wife and I are both approaching geriatric vintage, and one of us might have a heart attack or stroke one of these days.

Since all our cruising in the 20 years after 1946 was confined to the waters between Nantucket and Long Island Sound, we never felt the need for RDF once we had brought *Direction* safely home from Baddeck. With a good lead line we felt no need for a depth-sounder, either.

I never had the notion that it was unsportsmanlike to use radio aids; it was more a matter of inertia and indifference. If I needed them, then I'd get them. That was the case when I began making plans for a return to northern waters. I purchased a depth-sounder capable of reading down to 40 fathoms, more as an aid to navigation than for gunkholing into shallow harbors. Hiram Maxim made a direct-reading RDF for me out of a portable radio and an attached compass. He compensated with internal magnets for the deviation caused by the antenna.

I also became aware of the merits of loran and installed a DX Navigator for loran "A." This proved to be a joy and comfort, giving us good fixes in no-visibility situations anywhere in the Gulf of Maine or even Block Island Sound. In Nova Scotia and Cabot Strait, we can only get one line of position, but that is good enough in combination with our depth-sounder or RDF.

Years before they came on the market, I had a stainless steel radar reflector made for me by the New Haven Stove Repair

Company. I had it checked out by the skipper of the Block Island pilot boat, who reported that it returned a sharp pip to his radar screen. I carry this reflector always, at my port spreader.

Today I also have a portable "Fish Finder" depth-sounder, presented to me by my old friend Dr. Daniel Blain. It comes in very handy for gunkholing. On the keel of my dinghy I have installed a rubber clip of the type used to hold fishing rods. The transducer of the portable depth-sounder snaps into the clip, and I can send a crew member off in the dinghy to sound out a channel while I follow at a discreet distance in *Direction*. The set comes with a vacuum cup and clip so that I can also attach it to the hull of our aluminum canoe and take soundings from that, too.

So, bit by bit, the boat that sailed to Greenland without an engine, radio or other electronic aids, has gradually succumbed to the siren song of modern gadgets—except for radar—and by the summer of 1977 will have made a rather full swing in the other direction.

ON FUEL TANKS

IN A RECENT ISSUE of one of our most prestigious yachting magazines, the editor related an incident of having trouble with his diesel engine while cruising in Florida waters. The symptoms of the trouble were what he called "hunting" at 1000 rpm, and eventual stopping. This necessitated bleeding the injectors before the engine would run again. Now, one of the basic advantages of a diesel engine over gasoline is that once you start it, it never stops until you either turn it off or it runs out of fuel. It developed that the editor's engine had indeed run out of fuel, due to a fuel line clogged at the tank. I can't help but deplore the approach to designing boats that allows such a thing to happen in this enlightened age.

"Oh, the tank probably had dirty fuel," I can imagine someone saying. Perhaps that was the explanation, but tanks should be protected from dirty fuel. What do we have naval architects for, if not to design ways to prevent such failures? For over 30 years I have many times used fuel that was probably dirty—diesel oil from rusty old drums in some Newfoundland outport, and God only knows what else. Yet never have I experienced a clogged fuel line.

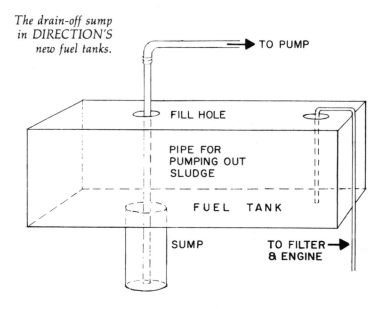

The drain-off sump in DIRECTION'S new fuel tanks.

TO PUMP

FILL HOLE

PIPE FOR
PUMPING OUT
SLUDGE

FUEL   TANK

SUMP

TO FILTER →
& ENGINE

My present stainless steel fuel tank has a sump *(see sketch)* located directly beneath the fill pipe. This sump is five inches in diameter, eight inches deep and projects down from the tank's bottom. As the motion of the boat sloshes the fuel around, any water or sludge in the tank eventually drops into the sump, which has no drain. Once a year I empty the sump through a one-inch copper tube inserted down the fill pipe. To the top of this tube, I attach a hand pump used for changing the engine lube oil, and pump the fuel from the sump into a glass container where I can see what I am getting. Usually there is some water and a good deal of sludge, but at last the fuel comes out clean—and I put my copper tube away for another year.

But that is not all. My fuel line to the engine comes out of the *top* of the tank, and is centrally located. The lower end is within an inch of the tank's bottom, but is nowhere near any edges or corners where sludge might accumulate. It leads to a large filter that has a cock for periodic draining, then to a second filter at the motor and eventually—by way of the lift pump—to the CAV high-pressure fuel pump. Except for the sump, which is my own invention, this setup has been in *Direction* since Walter Pinaud installed her first gasoline engine in 1945. If Walter Pinaud, way up in the wilds of Nova Scotia, was smart enough to develop a foolproof installation in 1945, why can't it be done by our present-day drawing board geniuses and boatyard mechanics?

Water tanks are another area where I depart from modern designers. In the frantic effort to keep weight low, tanks are installed in the bilge of the boat. They are often made an integral part of the boat, and even fabricated from smelly, foul-tasting plastic. The fill pipe often takes such a circuitous route that it is impossible ever to sound the tank to find out how much water is in it. The only way you know the tank is full is when the combination vent and overflow pipe spews water all over your upholstery—and eventually rots out your bulkhead. Just how foolish can you be?

Besides, sooner or later someone is going to fill your water tanks with gasoline or diesel oil, and then what do you do? And, there are other reasons you might need to drain your water tanks. The town water at Baddeck, Nova Scotia, occasionally contains sediment, and at other times is strongly treated with chlorine. I had not based *Direction* there very long before I decided to cart my own spring water for her tanks. With eight five-gallon jerricans I can carry 40 gallons of Bucklaw Mountain spring water in one trip with my car and nearly fill my 45-gallon stainless steel water tank. But how to remove the sediment already there? I finally dreamed up a simple, effective way.

With the tank three-quarters empty, I turn off the valve, disconnect the piping and go for a sail in a fresh breeze and a fair-sized sea. When I can hear the water sloshing against the baffle plates and sides of the tank, I open the valve and let the water drain into the bilge. Then I go from port tack to starboard and back again. That cleans my water tank and I have never had any problem with it since.

Peter Barlow took this photo of DIRECTION in 1958, when I just happened to be sailing single-handed. I nearly drove the cutter onto Fairfield Reef holding the "pose" while he read his light meter.

SINGLEHANDED SAILING

AUTHOR'S NOTE: Claud Worth, the renowned English yachting writer, whose word was law on boating matters around the turn of the century, wrote as early as 1910: "The charm of singlehanded cruising is not solitude but independence. A man may cruise with his wife if he is fortunate enough to have married one who loves the sea, or perhaps with a congenial companion, but he must be able to handle the vessel easily under all conditions when such assistance is not available." That has been my goal in fitting Direction *with roller-furling jibs, gallows frame and easily catted anchors.*

Because my first boat was a 20-foot cruising catboat I never was uneasy about singlehanded sailing or cruising. Until I got into trouble, I gave it no more thought than driving a car alone. I suppose I was the only student at Moses Brown School in Providence, Rhode Island (or anywhere, for that matter), to go to school by sailboat. It was on the occasion of my returning home to Rye, New York, one spring that I was becalmed off Charles Island in the late afternoon, and decided to go into Milford, Connecticut, for the night. Now my old Lathrop make-and-break one-cylinder engine was cranked with a bronze handle that retracted into the heavy flywheel when not in use. To grasp it, you pushed it in from the back of the flywheel with your index finger and pulled out the handle at the front. A spring made it snap back as soon as you let go.

199

In this case, the engine hung fire for some reason, then fired a-gain just as I stuck my index finger into the hole in the back of the flywheel for a second try at cranking. The flywheel turned and jammed my finger between it and the engine bed. There I was, trapped down in the bilge and, from the way it felt, with only half a finger left. There was no other human within several miles. Eventually, I extricated myself with no more injury than a blood blister on each side of the second joint of my finger. But it gave me pause. I never told my parents about the incident for fear some restriction might be imposed upon my singlehanded cruising.

On another occasion, I was on my way home from Chesapeake Bay via the old Delaware and Raritan Canal. It was late in the day when I locked out of the canal at New Brunswick, New Jersey. I knew that a lesser hurricane (or so I thought) was coming up the coast, so I dropped down to the mouth of the Raritan River and anchored for the night—out of the channel but well sheltered by marshes from any seas that might work in from Raritan Bay. My thought was that the storm would be over by morning when I could get a good northwest slant for the sail up the East River and eastward to my home port at Rye, New York.

Well, the hurricane arrived all right, but it was not the lesser one I was anticipating. I had no radio, nor would there have been any warning, in 1928, if I had. The weather bureau on top of the Whitehall Building on lower Manhattan clocked winds of 80 miles per hour. I sat up from 2:00 A.M. until dawn watching—as the tide rose and my sheltering marsh disappeared beneath the rising waves. The anchor held (a 50-pound kedge for a 20-foot catboat!), but from bearings on shore I could see we were dragging inch by inch through the soft mud, and that in a matter of hours we would be ashore. So I decided to return to New Brunswick at daylight and tie up just below the first lock until matters improved a bit.

The procedure for getting underway off a lee shore with a hand-cranked engine and no clutch consisted of shortening up scope on the anchor rode, leading it into the cockpit from the bowsprit chock, securing it and then going down into the bilge to crank the engine. Once the engine started, I dashed for the cockpit and, steering with the tiller against my hip, frantically struggled with both hands to break out the well-dug-in 50-pound kedge. Luckily there was still enough force in the wind so the boat did not override the anchor. But at that moment, as is so often the case, the unexpected happened. I got cramps in the muscles of my hands and could not release the anchor rode. I managed to get a turn on a cleat and free one hand which I pushed against the cabin bulkhead trying to straighten out my fingers, but the moment I curled them around the rode again, they cramped up once more in torturous pain.

At that moment the 50-pound kedge decided to break out of its own accord and we swung off the wind toward the lee riverbank. Even with the turn on the cleat I needed both hands to keep from losing the anchor rode, so I steered with my buttocks until we came to a bend in the river which led downwind. Meanwhile the anchor was trailing underneath the keel as the combination of wind and engine gave us a good turn of speed. Eventually we came to a bend in the river that headed us nearly upwind, and the boat slowed down enough so I could haul in the anchor inch by inch, up to the bowsprit chock-a-block. I arrived back at the first lock at New Brunswick pretty well bushed, but recovered after a hearty breakfast at a nearby diner.

Only once have I been in trouble singlehanding *Direction*. It was 1954 and Hurricane Carol was coming up the coast. I wanted to move *Direction* from Essex, Connecticut, to my hurricane mooring in the Branford River. I simply did not have time to round up a crew, so took off alone. I tied in a deep reef at Essex and proceeded downriver, then west toward Branford under reefed main, forestaysail and engine. Once out of the Connecticut River and heading westward along the shore, the east wind preceding the oncoming hurricane seemed deceptively mild so I unrolled first the jib and then the jibtopsail. We made marvelous time riding the flood tide, but then discretion began to surface, and I decided to roll up the, by then, surplus headsails; once again I got cramps in my finger muscles. Had anything gone adrift I would have been in serious trouble, but as it was, I simply waited and tried to relax, and eventually I succeeded in rolling up the topsail and the jib. This takes considerable doing in a breeze of wind as you pull in on the furling line, let out a bit more sheet, haul in some more on the furling line, all the while trying not to let the sail thrash around with slack sheets. My real trouble came rounding up to enter Branford Harbor when I had to sheet in the reefed mainsail. Every time I put any effort to it, my fingers became uncontrollable. It was rather frightening, but with the engine running I was in no real danger. Hurricane Carol arrived 18 hours later and I was still aboard *Direction*, but by that time we were as snug as could be, deep into the sheltered Branford River.

What I have described is mild compared to having a stroke, a coronary, or perhaps falling overboard, with your safety line dragging you along, and unable to get back aboard again. After Sam Wetherill lost his life by falling overboard from his boat while at anchor, I installed bronze step-handles on *Direction's* outboard rudder. Three are below the waterline, one just at it, and two above, all placed for ease in climbing aboard. Admittedly this may create drag, but I expect to come in last in Off Soundings races anyway, so who cares?

Having suggested by these incidents how risky it is to sail alone, even in Long Island Sound, let me add that it is also a lot of fun. With *Direction's* roller-furling jibs I am totally independent. I can sail alone, or with my wife, or with a bunch of landlubbers, and it makes no difference. I am not a slave to any crew. Also, I can go for a casual sail. You don't do that if it takes you 20 minutes to get under way and half an hour to furl sails and put the boat to bed again. But since I can get going in my 13½-ton cutter just as easily as in my old catboat, there were many times when we enjoyed even a half-hour sail from Essex, on the Connecticut River.

Many is the time I have set out alone in Long Island Sound, and when well out, lashed the tiller and set the headsails and let *Direction* head off toward the other side while I relaxed in the cabin or on deck basking in the sun with a book. Although I have yet to take *Direction* to sea alone, I would not hesitate to do so. It just happens that my family likes sailing as well as I do and there have been few occasions when I sailed alone.

ON LIVING ABOARD

"IT'S MORE important to own a decent boat than a decent house!"

The speaker was the late A. Duncan Seymour, a charter member of the Cruising Club of America and a classmate of Rockwell Kent's in the Columbia School of Architecture. He and his wife were at that moment our dinner guests in our newly purchased home which we were proudly displaying to him. It's possible that he forgot those words of wisdom almost as soon as he spoke them, but they have lingered with me ever since.

We had been living on the outer fringes of affluence and respectability ever since the Great Depression of the 1930's. Such establishment symbols as a good job and decent home had taken priority, with the result that we had gone along for 20 years cruising in our little catboat which had been built before the turn of the century and was now quite defintely showing her age.

Many people with possibly a stronger wanderlust or weaker ties to society had thrown respectability to the winds, given up jobs, sold homes and family possessions to live on a boat as nautical tramps roaming the world. Not me; I simply did not have the nerve.

However, Duncan Seymour's words preyed on my mind. That was why, within the year, I turned my dreams into reality and acquired *Direction*. But it was to be another 20 years before the prospect of retirement gave me the chance to do exactly as I pleased with my life. Meanwhile I had many opportunities to watch those bolder or with more affluence cope with the same dilemma. Irving and Exy Johnson are perhaps the best examples I know of a couple who made a life of cruising. Both were indoctrinated in the 1920's by Warwick Tomkins aboard his schooner, *Wander Bird*. Then, as newlyweds, a year or two later they searched Europe for a similar craft, finally finding one in England that became the first *Yankee*. They have since spent a lifetime roaming the seven seas. Thousands have dreamed the same dream.

The mode of living aboard includes for most of us, children. Our daughter, Diana, who has cruised with us from infancy, here appears to be enjoying a rainy day with her mother, at the helm. Thirty years later, with her deep-sea sailing husband, Jonathan Shattuck, she still finds time to cruise with us aboard DIRECTION.

Allen's Island

But for every Irving and Exy there are a hundred of lesser stature, who through lack of experience, money or plain common sense, are eliminated along the way. Perhaps it would be better if enticing cruising tales were never published to tempt the ill-prepared to flee from civilization. A few years ago the press headlined the loss of a schooner and several lives on Brigantine Shoals off Atlantic City, New Jersey.

"All the owner's possessions were on the schooner which could not be insured on account of its age," the newspaper reported. A co-worker at the plant where the owner was employed said the owner had spent six years refurbishing the schooner."

What was such an ancient vessel doing off Brigantine Shoals in January in the first place? How sad to see young lives lost and dreams shattered! But the urge for escape and adventure is so overwhelming that many of us prefer to sail on a shoestring than not sail at all, and some of us pay the ultimate price.

One day long ago I watched in helpless horror as my year-old daughter reached to touch the glowing wire of an electric heater. It happened so fast I could not move quickly enough to prevent it. The howls that resulted from this perfectly natural bit of experimentation indicated to me that she would never do it again. The sum total of being burned and surviving adds up to the first-hand experience we all acquire as we grow up. You and I today know the difference between wood and wool because at an early age we put them both to our mouths—which are more sensitive than our fingers—and learned the difference. It took only one lesson for my daughter to learn about "hot."

However, in the sheltered lives we so often lead today there are areas in which we never seem to learn proper respect. People without respect for medicine patronize quacks. People without

M.V.P.V.

The Bras d'Or Lakes, as seen from the graves of Dr. and Mrs. Alexander Graham Bell at the top of Bienn Breagh (Beautiful Mountain). To the right is the village of Baddeck sheltered by Kidston's Island. Right center St. Patricks Channel stretches off to the westward. To the left lies Grand Narrows dotted by the railroad bridge with the mountains near St. Peter's Canal across the "Big Lake" in the far distance. Washabuckt Mountain dominates the left center of the picture while Hunter's Mountain and Bucklaw Mountain may be recognized in the far distance (right center). The scraggly trees on the second island from the left mark the sanctuary for hundreds of nesting cormorants in nature's very own high-rise apartments.

Baddeck
Harbour

M.V.P.V.

205

Aerial view of the Washabuckt River.

respect—learned respect—for finance are targets for every chain letter and stock fraud, and sadly, people without respect for the sea, too often become the prey of Father Neptune and his trident.

Our situation with *Direction* was a compromise, a sort of have-your-cake-and-eat-it arrangement. Although for twenty years we never took her east of Cape Cod, she still had the capability of a circumnavigation. We were armchair world travelers, if you will. But with retirement in sight, we purchased the land on the Bras d'Or Lakes and sailed north, intending to use *Direcion* as our summer cottage.

Direction makes an ideal seagoing mobile home. Each year we arrive at the shipyard in Baddeck at the end of May to find her launched, sometimes with her mast in place and sometimes with it still on sawhorses, waiting for me to make some last-minute adjustments. Just being in that shipyard in the spring is a delight—not at all like City Island or even Essex, Connecticut. The cry of the bald eagles resting on Kidston Island across the harbor attracts our attention to father eagle soaring in the updrafts. A great blue heron fishes within 100 feet of us; yellow legs and sandpipers flit along the beach, and the small fry of a family of muskrats can be heard squeaking in their den under the logs of the wharf where we work. The sky is blue, the air is crisp and clean. *Bienn Bhreagh* (Gaelic for Beautiful Mountain), where the home of the late Alexander Graham Bell is situated, stands out across the water in the morning sunshine, while the mountains of Washabuckt, directly across the way, beckon us to our home anchorage. But we resist and relax. It is so pleasant fitting out in these surrounding that we sometimes take two weeks to complete the work. There's still a whole summer to relish the delights of Washabuckt.

If Washabuckt or the Bras d'Or Lakes should ever pall on us, there is Newfoundland only an overnight sail away. Oh, yes, I'm sure that Norway would be a grand place to cruise, but why go so far when the continental drift has obligingly slid a bit of Norway over to within 100 miles of our summer base? Dr. Paul Sheldon of Labrador fame once scornfully remarked, "Cruising in the Bras d'Or Lakes is no better than rowing in Central Park Lake." For his adventurous and intrepid spirit, this could well be so, but looking forward to our rapidly approaching old age, we have, on the Bras d'Or Lakes, all of the pleasures and few of the responsibilities of cruising.

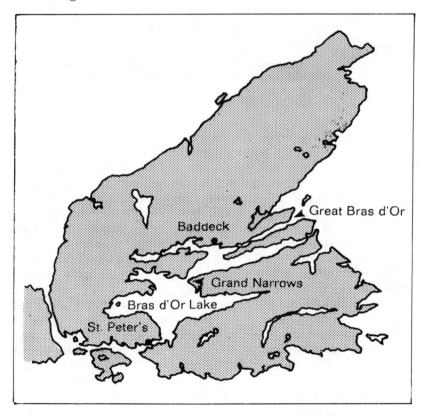

Johnson's Point, Branford, Connecticut.

On the land we purchased several years ago, we have a mail-box (Mailbox Cove), a parking space, a dinghy dock and, lately, a tent in which to store diesel oil, spring water, stove oil, kerosene, and all the sundry supplies that otherwise we'd have to travel to Baddeck to obtain. We have no house and don't plan to build one till we are too feeble to row out to *Direction*. A house would compete with *Direction* for time, affection and attention, and besides, perhaps we could not afford one. We like this setup so much that since our retirement we live aboard until early November with our diesel stove keeping us as warm and cozy as if we were living ashore in a "respectable" house.

Most sailors do not appear in print until they have made a circumnavigation or at least visited some exotic lands out of the reach of the ordinary person. Not so in my case! Here I chronicle a most commonplace existence. What glamour and adventure there may be, lies in the imagination. But let me assure you it has been a hell of a lot of fun and if by emulating me rather than Irving and Exy Johnson you avoid tragedy on Brigantine Shoals, this saga may have served some useful purpose.

CONCLUSION

IN THE LATE FALL of 1974 I was in Connecticut making a trial run in our 21-foot outboard-powered lobster boat, *Highland Heart,* while *Direction,* with her mast removed, was awaiting her turn to be hauled for the winter at Pinaud's yard in Baddeck.

Slowly we motored down the Patchogue River, passing marinas chock-a-block full of powerboats and sailboats, and continued out into Duck Island Roads, where we could open up and give *Highland Heart* her speed trials. She will never replace *Direction,* but as a second and trailerable yacht, she will get us out on Long Island Sound when we are in Connecticut, and hopefully to Florida in the wintertime. But that is not the point of this story.

Duck Island Roads has a special place in my heart that defies all reason. It is bleak and inhospitable, with two stark breakwaters running out at right angles to each other from Duck Island. It was built in the days of sail to provide a haven where coasting schooners could find shelter while awaiting favorable conditions for proceeding eastward or westward when the tide served. Fifty years ago, when I first anchored there, it was often used as such a refuge and it was common to enter of an evening and find two or three "hookers," as these schooners were called, at anchor, their skippers puffing away at their pipes while relaxing on the wheel box or coach roof.

It was a thrill to watch one of those graceful vessels ghosting in on a dying breeze, stemming a tide that had only recently turned foul, then rounding up, dropping her headsails, and letting go her anchor with a splash, followed by the rattle and clatter of chain paying out. Today, these are but memories, nearly lost in oblivion.

Similarly doomed to oblivion, had not David Higgins picked up his pen and made a record of it, is the ordinary fact that Higgins and another man, on a day in March, rowed a skiff down this very same Patchogue River, continued past Duck Island and across Long Island Sound to the narrow spit of beach that connects Orient Point to the rest of Long Island. They portaged across the spit and relaunched into Orient Harbour, whence they continued on their way to their destination at Shelter Island.

David Higgins was my grandfather's grandfather and the year was 1786. While it may seem foolhardy to you or me to row a skiff across Long Island Sound in March, for them it was perfectly reasonable, as there existed no other means of crossing the Sound. How I wish that my great-great-grandfather David Higgins had written a few more details of that trip, and of his life during the following 18 years as pastor of the little church at Hamburg Cove, just up the Connecticut River from Essex. But for him, the life around him was so familiar and commonplace that it was not worth recording, even 50 years later when he penned his memoirs.

Similarly the life and early days of *Direction* were so much taken for granted as to be skimmed over. Our viewpoints and our assumptions shift so imperceptibly through the years that, looking back only a decade, we can be jolted by the marked change in our circumstances or attitudes. Were it not for the evidence at hand in the concrete form of letters, cables and photographs, much of what life was like when *Direction* was new would be lost, even to those who were participants. New experiences quickly crowd out the old.

Hidden beneath the hard exterior shell of most of us, lurks a soul, tender, soft and vulnerable. In this often harsh and competitive world we soon learn to conceal it except in the presence of family and friends. Peggy Calnan and her husband Harry took a chance on being rebuffed when they wrote to a total stranger in Essex whose name they could not even remember. (You rarely speak to strangers if you live in New York City.) But their sense of history and the urge to preserve priceless documents prevailed, making it possible for those documents to be shared with you and me.

210

In faraway Cape Breton Island, where life is less competitive, that exterior shell is not quite so thick. People are friendly to strangers, so it was only natural for Joe MacLean to hurry home after seeing *Direction,* return with Edward L. Ayres' logbook, and present it to someone he had met for the first time just a half hour before. Joe is a sailor; he understands. When he was cleaning out Arthur Allen's studio and came across the tattered logbook, he sensed its value. He did not know at the time just what to do with it but he did feel it should not be destroyed.

And so, if my saga has been of interest or given you pleasure, please bear in mind that it was the instinct and imagination of many generous people like Joe, the Calnans, and Lewis Davis, cooperating with the Fates, that made it possible.

Like Coleridge's Ancient Mariner I have had a compulsion to tell my tale, but unlike the Wedding Guest, who "cannot choose but hear," you could have closed the book at any point and I would never have known the difference. Nevertheless, it has been a delight to have you aboard *Direction* for this gam.

Let's pour one more noggin before you leave. And let's raise a toast to Colin Archer, Billy Atkin, Sidney Miller, and Arthur Allen; and a special one to Lucian Cary, Sam Allen and, last but by no means least, to that controversial figure, Rockwell Kent.

THE END

1977

INDEX

215

This book was set by photocomposition in 10 point Caledonia with 2 points of leading by Brush-Mill Books, Inc., in Guilford, Connecticut; The book was printed at Lithocrafters, Inc., Chelsea, Michigan. Designer Kathleen A. Wells.